Java and J2EE

Dr.C.S. Pillai

B.S. Shakunthala

Published by

BONFRING®
Intellectual Integrity

Java and J2EE

9 789386 176615 >

ISBN 978-93-86176-61-5

Author

Dr.C.S. Pillai

B.S. Shakunthala

Bonfring

309, 2nd Floor, 5th Street Extension, Gandhipuram,

Coimbatore-641 012.

Tamilnadu, India.

E-mail: info@bonfring.org

Website: www.bonfring.org

Phone: 0422 4213231

Preface

The importance of **Java and J2EE** is well known in various engineering fields. The book uses plain, lucid language to explain fundamental of this subject .This book provides logical method of explaining various complicated concepts and stepwise methods to explain the important topics.

Each chapter is well supported with necessary illustrations, practical examples and solved problems.

All care has been take care to make students comfortable in understanding the basic concepts of the subject.

We wish to express our thanks to all those who helped in making this book a reality.

We wish to thank the publisher and the entire team who have taken immense pain to get this book in time with quality printing.

Dr.C.S. Pillai

B.S. Shakunthala

Acknowledgement

Unit	Contents	Page No

UNIT-1

INTRODUCTION TO JAVA

1.1. Introduction

Since the invention of the computer, many approaches of program development have evolved. These include modular programming, top-down programming, bottom-up programming and structured programming. The primary motivation in each case has been the concern to handle the increasing complexity of programs to be reliable and maintainable. These techniques became popular among programmers in 1970s and 1980s.

Due to the popularity of C language, structured programming became very popular and was the main technique of the 1980s. Later this technique also failed to show the desired performance in terms of maintainability, reusability and reliability.

As a result of this realization, a new methodology known as Object oriented programming emerges. This approach to program organization and development attempts to eliminate some of the pitfalls of conventional programming by incorporating the best of the structured programming features with several powerful new concepts. This approach speeds the development of new programs, and, if properly used, improves the maintenance, reusability, and modifiability of software. So, the major concern for all of us is to know what it is. What are the main features of this approach? How is it better than other approaches? What are the languages which support its various features? In this unit, we will start with a brief discussion of the manner in which different languages have been developed so as to understand where an Object Oriented programming language fits in.

1.2. Objectives

After going through this unit, you should be able to

- find the importance of OO approach;
- define the basic concepts of OO approach;
- Learn about the Java Runtime Environment and how a Java program is created, compiled, and run.
- Learn how to download, install, and set up the Java Development Kit Standard Edition.
- Learn how to create a simple Java program
- Understand Java's basic syntax rules, including statements, blocks, and comments.

- Declare variables; construct statements using variables and literal (constant) values.
- Become familiar with the primitive data types, as well as the String class.
- Understand many of Java's operators and the concept of operator precedence.
- Understand the rules that apply when data is converted from one type to another.

1.3. Java and Java Applications

Java is a **programming language** and a **platform. Platform:** Any hardware or software environment in which a program runs, known as a platform. Since Java has its own Runtime Environment (JRE) and API, it is called platform According to Sun, 3 billion devices run java. There are many devices where java is currently used. Some of them are as follows:

- Desktop Applications such as acrobat reader, media player, antivirus etc.
- Web Applications such as irctc.co.in, javatpoint.com etc.
- Enterprise Applications such as banking applications.
- Mobile
- Embedded System
- Smart Card, Robotics Games etc.

Types of Java Applications: There are mainly 4 types of applications that can be created using java:

1. **Standalone Application:** It is also known as desktop application or window-based application. An application that we need to install on every machine such as media player, antivirus etc. AWT and Swing are used in java for creating standalone applications.
2. **Web Application:** An application that runs on the server side and creates dynamic page, is called web application. Currently, servlet, jsp, struts, jsf etc. technologies are used for creating web applications in java.
3. **Enterprise Application:** An application that is distributed in nature, such as banking applications etc. It has the advantage of high level security, load balancing and clustering. In java, EJB is used for creating enterprise applications.
4. **Mobile Application:** An application that is created for mobile devices. Currently Android and Java ME are used for creating mobile applications.

1.4. Java Development Kit (JDK)

JDK is an acronym for Java Development Kit. It physically exists. It contains JRE + development tools.

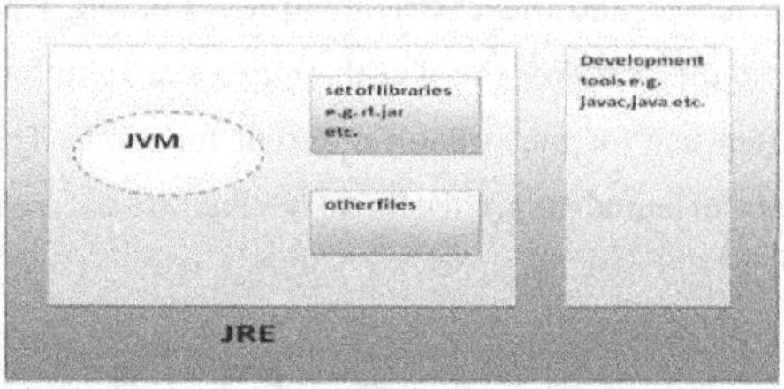

JDK

1.5. JVM , JRE

JVM (Java Virtual Machine) is an abstract machine. It is a specification that provides runtime environment in which java byte code can be executed. JVMs are available for many hardware and software platforms. JVM, JRE and JDK are platform dependent because configuration of each OS differs. But, Java is platform independent. The JVM performs following main tasks:

- Loads code.
- Verifies code.
- Executes code.
- Provides runtime environment.

JRE is an acronym for Java Runtime Environment. It is used to provide runtime environment. It is the implementation of JVM. It physically exists. It contains set of libraries + other files that JVM uses at runtime.

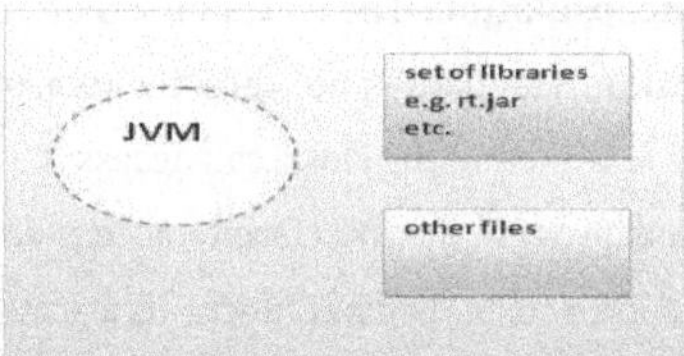

JRE

1.6. Object-Oriented Programming

The world and its applications are not organized as functions and values separate from one another. The problem solvers do not think about the world in this manner. They always deal with their problems by concentrating on the **objects**, their **characteristics** and **behavior**.

The *world is Object Oriented,* and Object Oriented programming expresses programs in the ways that model how people perceive the world. *Figure* shows different real world objects around us which we often use for performing different functions. This shows that problem solving using the objects oriented approach is very close to our real life problem solving techniques.

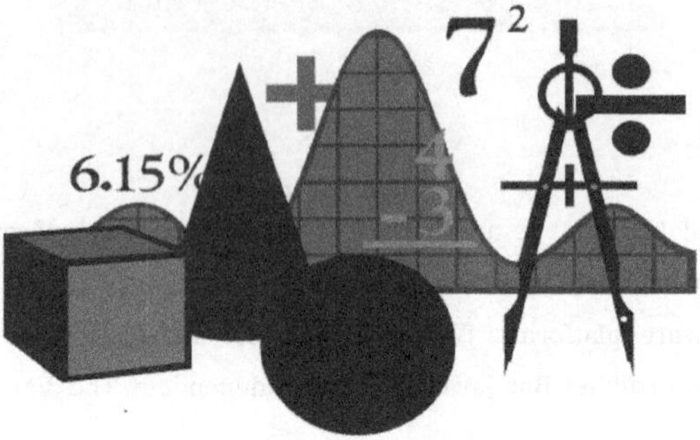

Real World Objects

The basic difference in Object Oriented programming **(OOP)** is that the program is organized around the data being operated upon rather than the operations performed. The basic idea behind OOP is to *combine both, data and its functions* that operate on the data into a single unit called **object**. Now in our next section, we will learn about the basic concepts used extensively in the Object Oriented approach.

Four Corner Stone's of OOPS

Data abstraction and encapsulation: The wrapping up of data and functions into a single unit is known as **encapsulation**. The data is not directly accessible to the outside world and only the functions, which are wrapped in the class, can access it. Functions are accessible to the outside world. These functions provide the interface to access data. If one wants to modify the data of an object, s/he should know exactly what functions are available to interact with it. This insulation of the data from direct access by the program is known as **data hiding.**

Abstraction: refers to the act of representing essential features without including the background details to distinguish objects/ functions from other objects/functions. In case of structured programming, **functional abstraction** was provided by telling, **which task is performed by function and hiding how that task is performed**. A step further, in the Object Oriented approach, classes use the concept of **data abstraction.** With data abstraction, data structures can be used without having to be concerned about the exact details of implementation. As in case of built-in data types like integer, floating point, etc. The programmer only knows about the various operations which can be performed on these data types, but how these operations are carried out by the hardware or software is hidden from the programmer. Similarly in Object Oriented approach, classes act as **abstract data types**. Classes are defined as a set of attributes and functions to operate on these attributes. They encapsulate all the essential properties of the objects that are to be created.

Inheritance: Inheritance is the process by which objects of one class acquire the properties of objects of another class in the hierarchy. For example, the scooter is a type of the class two-wheelers, which is again a type of (or kind of) the class motor vehicles. The principle behind inheritance is that the derived class shares common characteristics with the class from which it is derived. New classes can be built from the existing classes. It means that we can add additional features to an existing class without modifying it. The new class is referred as **derived class** or **sub class** and the original class is known as **base class** or **superclass**. Therefore, the concept of inheritance provides the idea of **reusability.** This inheritance mechanism allows the programmer to reuse a class that is made almost, but not exactly, similar to the required one by adding a few more features to it.

Polymorphism: Polymorphism means **the ability to take more than one form of the same property.** For example, consider an addition operation. It shows a different behaviour in different types of data. For two numbers, it will generate a sum. The numbers may integers or float. Thus the addition for integers is different from the addition to floats.

1.7. Java Features

There is given many features of java. They are also known as java buzzwords.

- Object-Oriented
- Platform independent
- Simple
- Secured
- Architecture neutral
- Portable
- Robust
- Multithreaded
- Interpreted
- High Performance

- Distributed
- Dynamic

Object Oriented: In Java, everything is an Object. Java can be easily extended since it is based on the Object model.

Platform independent: Unlike many other programming languages including C and C++, when Java is compiled, it is not compiled into platform specific machine, rather into platform independent byte code. This byte code is distributed over the web and interpreted by virtual Machine (JVM) on whichever platform it is being run.

Simple: Java is designed to be easy to learn. If you understand the basic concept of OOP Java would be easy to master.

Secure: With Java's secure feature it enables to develop virus-free, tamper-free systems. Authentication techniques are based on public-key encryption.

Architectural-neutral: Java compiler generates an architecture-neutral object file format which makes the compiled code to be executable on many processors, with the presence of Java runtime system.

Portable: Being architectural-neutral and having no implementation dependent aspects of the specification makes Java portable. Compiler in Java is written in ANSI C with a clean portability boundary which is a POSIX subset.

Robust: Java makes an effort to eliminate error prone situations by emphasizing mainly on compile time error checking and runtime checking.

Multithreaded: With Java's multithreaded feature it is possible to write programs that can do many tasks simultaneously. This design feature allows developers to construct smoothly running interactive applications.

Interpreted: Java byte code is translated on the fly to native machine instructions and is not stored anywhere. The development process is more rapid and analytical since the linking is an incremental and light weight process.

High Performance: With the use of Just-In-Time compilers, Java enables high performance.

Distributed: Java is designed for the distributed environment of the internet.

Dynamic: Java is considered to be more dynamic than C or C++ since it is designed to adapt to an evolving environment. Java programs can carry extensive amount of run-time information that can be used to verify and resolve accesses to objects on run-time.

1.8. Simple Java Program

```
class Simple{
   public static void main(String args[]){
    System.out.println("Hello Java");
   }
}
```

Save this file as **Simple.java**

To compile:javac imple.java

To execute:java Simple

Here is the meaning of class, public, static, void, main, String[], System.out.println().

- **class** keyword is used to declare a class in java.
- **public** keyword is an access modifier which represents visibility, it means it is visible to all.
- **static** is a keyword, if we declare any method as static, it is known as static method.
- The core advantage of static method is that there is no need to create object to invoke the static method. The main method is executed by the JVM, so it doesn't require to
- create object to invoke the main method. So it saves memory.
- **void** is the return type of the method, it means it doesn't return any value.
- **main** represents startup of the program.
- **String[] args** is used for command line argument.
- **System.out.println ()** is used print statement.

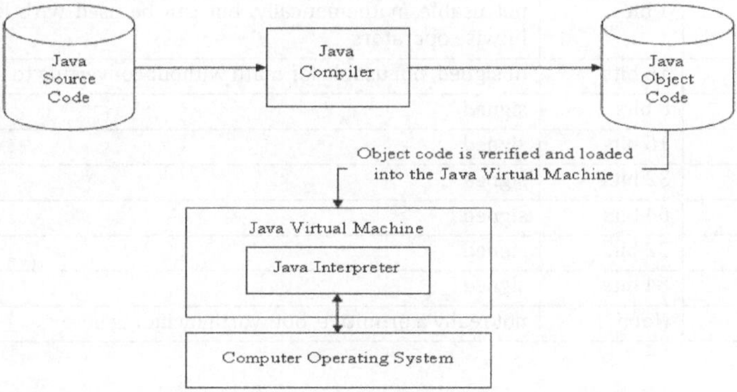

1.9. Data Types and Other Tokens

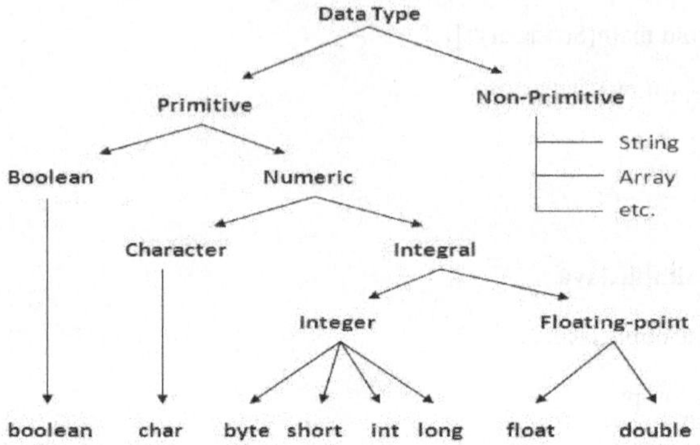

The primitive data types store single values at some memory location that the compiler selects and maps to the variable name you declared.

Primitive values are not objects - they do not have fields or methods.

A primitive value is stored at the named location, while an object is accessed using a reference.

An object reference variable does not store the object's data directly - it stores a reference to the block of data, which is somewhere else in memory (technically, the reference stores the memory address of the object, but you never get to see or use the address).

Primitives Data Types		
Primitive Type	**Storage Size**	**Comments**
boolean	1 bit	not usable mathematically, but can be used with logical and bitwise operators
char	16 bits	unsigned, not usable for math without converting to int
byte	8 bits	signed
short	16 bits	signed
int	32 bits	signed
long	64 bits	signed
float	32 bits	signed
double	64 bits	signed
void	None	not really a primitive, but worth including here

Object Data Types

Objects can be data, which can be stored in variables, passed to methods, or returned from methods.

References

As we will see later, objects are stored differently than primitives. An object variable stores a *reference* to the object (the object is located at some other memory location, and the reference is something like a memory address).

Text Strings

A sequence of text, such as a name, an error message, etc., is known as a *string*. In Java, the String class is used to hold a sequence of text characters.

A String Object

- Is accessed through a reference, since it is an object.
- Has a number of useful methods, for case-sensitive or case-insensitive comparisons, obtaining substrings, determining the number of characters, converting to upper or lower case, etc.
- Is immutable; that is, once created it cannot be changed (but you can make your variable reference a different String object at any time).

Literal Values

A value typed into your code is called a *literal* value.

The compiler makes certain assumptions about literals:

- True and false are literal boolean values.
- Null is a literal reference to nothing (for objects).
- A numeric value with no decimal places becomes an int, unless it is immediately assigned into a variable of a smaller type and falls within the valid range for that type.
- A value with decimal places becomes a double.
- To store a text character, you can put apostrophes around the character.

Code	Effect
char e = 'X';	Creates a 16-bit variable to hold the Unicode value for the uppercase X character.

You can add modifiers to values to instruct the compiler what type of value to create (note that all the modifiers described below can use either uppercase or lowercase letters).

Modifying Prefixes Enable you to use a Different Number Base

Prefix	Effect
0X *or* 0x	A base 16 value; the extra digits can be either uppercase or lowercase, as in char c = 0x1b;
0	A base 8 value, as in int i = 0765;

Note: using these prefixes will always result in number that is considered positive (so that 0x7F for a byte would be OK, but 0x80 would not, since the latter would have a value of 128, outside the range of byte).Also note that a long value would need the L modifier as discussed below.

Modifying Suffixes Create a Value of a Different Type than the Default

Suffix	Effect
L *or* l	a long value (uses 64 bits of storage), as in long l = 1234567890123456L;
	Note: An int value will always implicitly be promoted to a long when required, but the reverse is not true; the above notation is necessary because the literal value is larger than 32 bits
F *or* f	A float value, as in float f = 3.7F;

Escape Sequences for Character Values

There are a number of *escape sequences* that are used for special characters:

Escape Sequence	Resulting Character
\b	Backspace
\f	Form feed
\n	Linefeed character - note that it produces exactly one character, Unicode 10 (\u000A in hex)
\r	Carriage return
\t	Tab
\"	Quote mark
\'	Apostrophe
****	Backslash
\uNNNN	Unicode value, where N is a base 16 digit from 0 through F; valid values are \u0000 through \uFFFF
\NNN	Value expressed in octal; ranging from \000 to \377

The escape sequences can either be used for single characters or within strings of text:

```
char c = '\u1234';
System.out.println("\t\tHello\n\t\tWorld");
```

1.10. Variables, Arrays

Variable is name of reserved area allocated in memory.

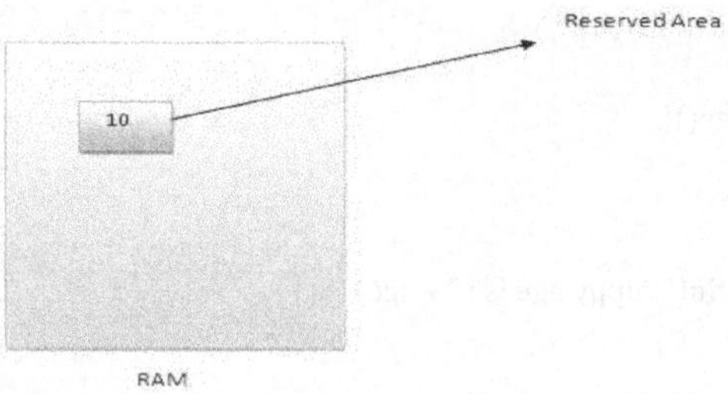

int data=50; //Here data is variable

Types of Variable

There are three types of variables in java

1) local variable
2) instance variable
3) static variable

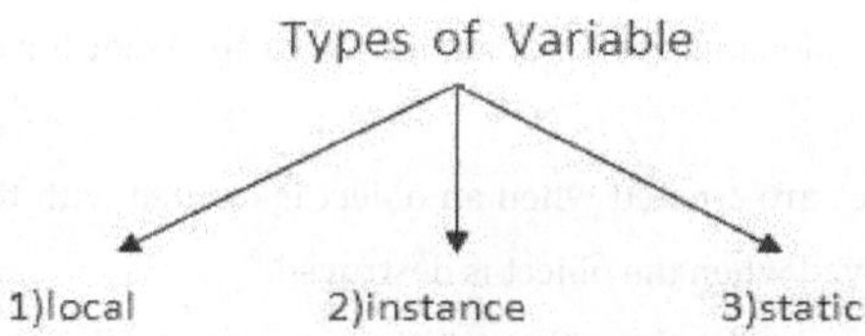

Local Variables

- Local variables are declared in methods, constructors, or blocks.
- Local variables are created when the method, constructor or block is entered and the variable will be destroyed once it exits the method, constructor or block.
- Access modifiers cannot be used for local variables.
- Local variables are visible only within the declared method, constructor or block.
- Local variables are implemented at stack level internally.
- There is no default value for local variables so local variables should be declared and an initial value should be assigned before the first use.

Example

Here, *age* is a local variable. This is defined inside *pupAge()* method and its scope is limited to this method only.

```
public class Test{
  public void pupAge(){
    int age = 0;
    age = age + 7;
    System.out.println("Puppy age is : " + age);
  }
  public static void main(String args[]){
    Test test = new Test();
    test.pupAge();
  }
}
```

Instance Variables

- Instance variables are declared in a class, but outside a method, constructor or any block.
- When a space is allocated for an object in the heap, a slot for each instance variable value is created.
- Instance variables are created when an object is created with the use of the keyword 'new' and destroyed when the object is destroyed.
- Instance variables hold values that must be referenced by more than one method, constructor or block, or essential parts of an object's state that must be present throughout the class.
- Instance variables can be declared in class level before or after use.
- Access modifiers can be given for instance variables.
- The instance variables are visible for all methods, constructors and block in the class. Normally, it is recommended to make these variables private (access level). However visibility for subclasses can be given for these variables with the use of access modifiers.
- Instance variables have default values. For numbers the default value is 0, for Booleans it is false and for object references it is null. Values can be assigned during the declaration or within the constructor.

- Instance variables can be accessed directly by calling the variable name inside the class. However within static methods and different class (when instance variables are given accessibility) should be called using the fully qualified name.
  Object Reference. VariableName.

Example

```
import java.io.*;
  public class Employee{
    // this instance variable is visible for any child class.
    public String name;
    // salary  variable is visible in Employee class only.
    private double salary;
    // The name variable is assigned in the constructor.
    public Employee (String empName){
      name = empName;
    }
    // The salary variable is assigned a value.
    public void setSalary(double empSal){
      salary = empSal;
    }
    // This method prints the employee details.
    public void printEmp(){
      System.out.println("name  : " + name );
      System.out.println("salary :" + salary);
    }
    public static void main(String args[]){
      Employee empOne = new Employee("Ransika");
      empOne.setSalary(1000);
      empOne.printEmp();
    }
  }
```

Class/Static Variables

- Class variables also known as static variables are declared with the *static* keyword in a class, but outside a method, constructor or a block.

- There would only be one copy of each class variable per class, regardless of how many objects are created from it.
- Static variables are rarely used other than being declared as constants. Constants are variables that are declared as public/private, final and static. Constant variables never change from their initial value.
- Static variables are stored in static memory. It is rare to use static variables other than declared final and used as either public or private constants.
- Static variables are created when the program starts and destroyed when the program stops.
- Visibility is similar to instance variables. However, most static variables are declared public since they must be available for users of the class.
- Default values are same as instance variables. For numbers, the default value is 0; for Booleans, it is false; and for object references, it is null. Values can be assigned during the declaration or within the constructor. Additionally values can be assigned in special static initializer blocks.
- Static variables can be accessed by calling with the class name. ***ClassName.VariableName.***
- When declaring class variables as public static final, then variables names (constants) are all in upper case. If the static variables are not public and final the naming syntax is the same as instance and local variables.

Example

```
import java.io.*;
public class Employee{
  // salary variable is a private static variable
  private static double salary;
  // DEPARTMENT is a constant
  public static final String DEPARTMENT = "Development ";
  public static void main(String args[]){
    salary = 1000;
    System.out.println(DEPARTMENT+"average salary:"+salary);
  }}
```

Arrays: Java provides a data structure, the **array**, which stores a fixed-size sequential collection of elements of the same type. An array is used to store a collection of data, but it is often more useful to think of an array as a collection of variables of the same type.

Instead of declaring individual variables, such as number0, number1, ..., and number99, you declare one array variable such as numbers and use numbers[0], numbers[1], and ..., numbers[99] to represent individual variables.

Declaring Array Variables: To use an array in a program, you must declare a variable to reference the array, and you must specify the type of array the variable can reference. Here is the syntax for declaring an array variable:

dataType[] arrayRefVar; // **preferred way**.

or

dataType arrayRefVar[]; // **works but not preferred way.**

Note: The style **dataType[] arrayRefVar** is preferred. The style **dataType arrayRefVar[]** comes from the C/C++ language and was adopted in Java to accommodate C/C++ programmers.

Example

The following code snippets are examples of this syntax:

double[] myList; // **preferred way.**

or

double myList[]; // **works but not preferred way.**

Creating Arrays

You can create an array by using the new operator with the following syntax:

arrayRefVar = new dataType[arraySize];

The above statement does two things:

- It creates an array using new dataType[arraySize];
- It assigns the reference of the newly created array to the variable arrayRefVar.

Declaring an array variable, creating an array, and assigning the reference of the array to the variable can be combined in one statement, as shown below:

dataType[] arrayRefVar = new dataType[arraySize];

Alternatively you can create arrays as follows:

dataType[] arrayRefVar = {value0, value1, ..., valuek};

The array elements are accessed through the **index**. Array indices are 0-based; that is, they start from 0 to **arrayRefVar.length-1**.

Example

Following statement declares an array variable, myList, creates an array of 10 elements of double type and assigns its reference to myList:

double[] myList = new double[10];

Following picture represents array myList. Here, myList holds ten double values and the indices are from 0 to 9.

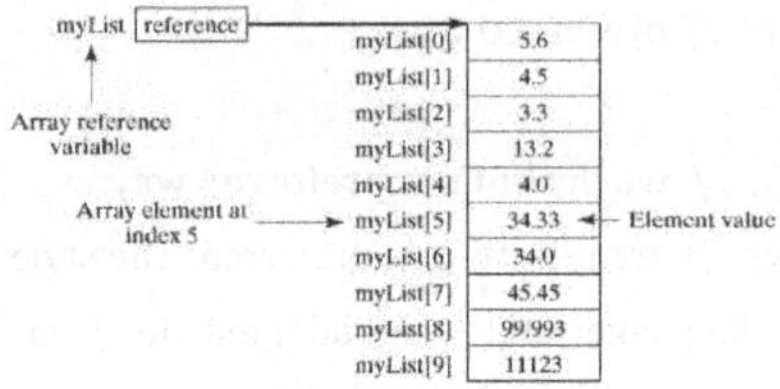

Example

Here is a complete example of showing how to create, initialize and process arrays:

```
public class TestArray {
  public static void main(String[] args) {
    double[] myList = {1.9, 2.9, 3.4, 3.5};
    // Print all the array elements
    for (int i = 0; i < myList.length; i++) {
      System.out.println(myList[i] + " ");
    }
    // Summing all elements
    double total = 0;
    for (int i = 0; i < myList.length; i++) {
      total += myList[i];
    }
    System.out.println("Total is " + total);
    // Finding the largest element
    double max = myList[0];
    for (int i = 1; i < myList.length; i++) {
      if (myList[i] > max) max = myList[i]; }
    System.out.println("Max is " + max);
  }
}
```

1.11. Creating and Destroying Objects

We know that class provides the blueprints for objects. So basically an object is created from a class. In Java, the **new** key word is used to create new objects. There are three steps when creating an object from a class:

- **Declaration:** A variable declaration with a variable name with an object type.
- **Instantiation:** The 'new' key word is used to create the object.
- **Initialization:** The 'new' keyword is followed by a call to a constructor. This call initializes the new object.

Example of creating an object is given below:

```
public class Puppy{
  public Puppy(String name){
    // This constructor has one parameter, name.
    System.out.println("Passed Name is :" + name );
  }
  public static void main(String []args){
    // Following statement would create an object myPuppy
    Puppy myPuppy = new Puppy( "tommy" );
  }
}
```

Destroying the object in java: java performs carbagge collection by itself no need to so it manually.

1.12. Access Specifiers

Access specifers/Modifiers are keywords that you add to those definitions to change their meanings. The Java language has a wide variety of modifiers, including the following:

- Java Access Modifiers.
- Non Access Modifiers.

To use a modifier, you include its keyword in the definition of a class, method, or variable. The modifier precedes the rest of the statement.

Java Access Modifiers: Java provides a number of access modifiers to set access levels for classes, variables, methods and constructors. The four access levels are:

- Visible to the package. the default. **No modifiers are needed.**
- Visible to the class only **(private).**

- Visible to the world **(public).**
- Visible to the package and all subclasses **(protected).**

Default Access Modifier - No Keyword

Default access modifier means we do not explicitly declare an access modifier for a class, field, method, etc.

A variable or method declared without any access control modifier is available to any other class in the same package.

The fields in an interface are implicitly public static final and the methods in an interface are by default public.

Example

Variables and methods can be declared without any modifiers, as in the following examples:

```
String version = "1.5.1";
boolean processOrder() {
  return true;
}
```

Private Access Modifier - private

Methods, Variables and Constructors that are declared private can only be accessed within the declared class itself.

Private access modifier is the most restrictive access level. Class and interfaces cannot be private.

Variables that are declared private can be accessed outside the class if public getter methods are present in the class.

Using the private modifier is the main way that an object encapsulates itself and hide data from the outside world.

Example

The following class uses private access control:

```
public class Logger {
  private String format;
  public String getFormat() {
```

```
        return this.format;
    }
    public void setFormat(String format) {
        this.format = format;
    }
}
```

Public Access Modifier - Public

A class, method, constructor, interface etc declared public can be accessed from any other class. Therefore fields, methods, blocks declared inside a public class can be accessed from any class belonging to the Java Universe.

However if the public class we are trying to access is in a different package, then the public class still need to be imported.

Because of class inheritance, all public methods and variables of a class are inherited by its subclasses.

Example

The following function uses public access control:

```
public static void main(String[] arguments) {
    // ...
}
```

The main() method of an application has to be public. Otherwise, it could not be called by a Java interpreter (such as java) to run the class.

Protected Access Modifier - Protected

Variables, methods and constructors which are declared protected in a super class can be accessed only by the subclasses in other package or any class within the package of the protected members' class.

The protected access modifier cannot be applied to class and interfaces. Methods, fields can be declared protected, however methods and fields in a interface cannot be declared protected.

Protected access gives the subclass a chance to use the helper method or variable, while preventing a nonrelated class from trying to use it.

Example

The following parent class uses protected access control, to allow its child class override openSpeaker() method:

```
class AudioPlayer {
  protected boolean openSpeaker(Speaker sp) {
    // implementation details
  }
}
class StreamingAudioPlayer {
  boolean openSpeaker(Speaker sp) {
    // implementation details
  }
}
```

Non Access Modifiers

Java provides a number of non-access modifiers to achieve many other functionality.

- The **static** modifier for creating class methods and variables
- The **final** modifier for finalizing the implementations of classes, methods, and variables.
- The **abstract** modifier for creating abstract classes and methods.
- The **synchronized** and **volatile** modifiers, which are used for threads.

1.13. Operators and Expressions

Java provides a rich set of operators to manipulate variables.

We can divide all the Java operators into the following groups:

- Arithmetic Operators
- Relational Operators
- Bitwise Operators
- Logical Operators
- Assignment Operators
- Misc Operators

The Arithmetic Operators

Arithmetic operators are used in mathematical expressions in the same way that they are used in algebra. The following table lists the arithmetic operators:

Assume integer variable A holds 10 and variable B holds 20, then:

Operator	Description	Example
+	Addition - Adds values on either side of the operator	A + B will give 30
-	Subtraction - Subtracts right hand operand from left hand operand	A - B will give -10
*	Multiplication - Multiplies values on either side of the operator	A * B will give 200
/	Division - Divides left hand operand by right hand operand	B / A will give 2
%	Modulus - Divides left hand operand by right hand operand and returns remainder	B % A will give 0
++	Increment - Increases the value of operand by 1	B++ gives 21
--	Decrement - Decreases the value of operand by 1	B-- gives 19

The following simple example program demonstrates the arithmetic operators.

```
public class Test {
  public static void main(String args[]) {
    int a = 10;
    int b = 20;
    int c = 25;
    int d = 25;
    System.out.println("a + b = " + (a + b) );
    System.out.println("a - b = " + (a - b) );
    System.out.println("a * b = " + (a * b) );
    System.out.println("b / a = " + (b / a) );
    System.out.println("b % a = " + (b % a) );
    System.out.println("c % a = " + (c % a) );
    System.out.println("a++   = " + (a++) );
    System.out.println("b--   = " + (a--) );
    // Check the difference in d++ and ++d
    System.out.println("d++   = " + (d++) );
    System.out.println("++d   = " + (++d) );
  }
}
```

The Relational Operators

There are following relational operators supported by Java language. Assume variable A holds 10 and variable B holds 20, then:

Operator	Description	Example
==	Checks if the values of two operands are equal or not, if yes then condition becomes true.	(A == B) is not true.
!=	Checks if the values of two operands are equal or not, if values are not equal then condition becomes true.	(A != B) is true.
>	Checks if the value of left operand is greater than the value of right operand, if yes then condition becomes true.	(A > B) is not true.
<	Checks if the value of left operand is less than the value of right operand, if yes then condition becomes true.	(A < B) is true.
>=	Checks if the value of left operand is greater than or equal to the value of right operand, if yes then condition becomes true.	(A >= B) is not true.
<=	Checks if the value of left operand is less than or equal to the value of right operand, if yes then condition becomes true.	(A <= B) is true.

The following simple example program demonstrates the relational operators.

```
public class Test {
 public static void main(String args[]) {
  int a = 10;
  int b = 20;
  System.out.println("a == b = " + (a == b) );
  System.out.println("a != b = " + (a != b) );
  System.out.println("a > b = " + (a > b) );
  System.out.println("a < b = " + (a < b) );
  System.out.println("b >= a = " + (b >= a) );
  System.out.println("b <= a = " + (b <= a) );
 }
}
```

The Bitwise Operators

Java defines several bitwise operators, which can be applied to the integer types, long, int, short, char, and byte.

Bitwise operator works on bits and performs bit-by-bit operation.

Assume if a = 60; and b = 13; now in binary format they will be as follows:

a = 0011 1100

b = 0000 1101

----

a&b = 0000 1100

a|b = 0011 1101

a^b = 0011 0001

~a = 1100 0011

The following table lists the bitwise operators: Assume integer variable A holds 60 and variable B holds 13 then:

Operator	Description	Example
&	Binary AND Operator copies a bit to the result if it exists in both operands.	(A & B) will give 12 which is 0000 1100
|	Binary OR Operator copies a bit if it exists in either operand.	(A | B) will give 61 which is 0011 1101
^	Binary XOR Operator copies the bit if it is set in one operand but not both.	(A ^ B) will give 49 which is 0011 0001
~	Binary Ones Complement Operator is unary and has the effect of 'flipping' bits.	(~A) will give -61 which is 1100 0011 in 2's complement form due to a signed binary number.
<<	Binary Left Shift Operator. The left operands value is moved left by the number of bits specified by the right operand.	A << 2 will give 240 which is 1111 0000
>>	Binary Right Shift Operator. The left operands value is moved right by the number of bits specified by the right operand.	A >> 2 will give 15 which is 1111
>>>	Shift right zero fill operator. The left operands value is moved right by the number of bits specified by the right operand and shifted values are filled up with zeros.	A >>>2 will give 15 which is 0000 1111

The following simple example program demonstrates the bitwise operators.

```
public class Test {
  public static void main(String args[]) {
    int a = 60;        /* 60 = 0011 1100 */
    int b = 13;        /* 13 = 0000 1101 */
    int c = 0;
    c = a & b;     /* 12 = 0000 1100 */
    System.out.println("a & b = " + c );
```

```
    c = a | b;     /* 61 = 0011 1101 */
    System.out.println("a | b = " + c );
    c = a ^ b;     /* 49 = 0011 0001 */
    System.out.println("a ^ b = " + c );
    c = ~a;        /*-61 = 1100 0011 */
    System.out.println("~a = " + c );
    c = a << 2;   /* 240 = 1111 0000 */
    System.out.println("a << 2 = " + c );
    c = a >> 2;   /* 215 = 1111 */
    System.out.println("a >> 2  = " + c );
    c = a >>> 2;    /* 215 = 0000 1111 */
    System.out.println("a >>> 2 = " + c );
  }
}
```

The Logical Operators

The following table lists the logical operators: Assume Boolean variables A holds true and variable B holds false, then:

Operator	Description	Example
&&	Called Logical AND operator. If both the operands are non-zero, then the condition becomes true.	(A && B) is false.
||	Called Logical OR Operator. If any of the two operands are non-zero, then the condition becomes true.	(A || B) is true.
!	Called Logical NOT Operator. Use to reverses the logical state of its operand. If a condition is true then Logical NOT operator will make false.	!(A && B) is true.

The following simple example program demonstrates the logical operators.

```
public class Test {
 public static void main(String args[]) {
   boolean a = true;
   boolean b = false;
   System.out.println("a && b = " + (a&&b));
   System.out.println("a || b = " + (a||b) );
   System.out.println("!(a && b) = " + !(a && b));
 }
}
```

The Assignment Operators

There are following assignment operators supported by Java language:

Operator	Description	Example
=	Simple assignment operator, Assigns values from right side operands to left side operand	C = A + B will assign value of A + B into C
+=	Add AND assignment operator, It adds right operand to the left operand and assign the result to left operand	C += A is equivalent to C = C + A
-=	Subtract AND assignment operator, It subtracts right operand from the left operand and assign the result to left operand	C -= A is equivalent to C = C - A
*=	Multiply AND assignment operator, It multiplies right operand with the left operand and assign the result to left operand	C *= A is equivalent to C = C * A
/=	Divide AND assignment operator, It divides left operand with the right operand and assign the result to left operand	C /= A is equivalent to C = C / A
%=	Modulus AND assignment operator, It takes modulus using two operands and assign the result to left operand	C %= A is equivalent to C = C % A
<<=	Left shift AND assignment operator	C <<= 2 is same as C = C << 2
>>=	Right shift AND assignment operator	C >>= 2 is same as C = C >> 2
&=	Bitwise AND assignment operator	C &= 2 is same as C = C & 2
^=	bitwise exclusive OR and assignment operator	C ^= 2 is same as C = C ^ 2
|=	bitwise inclusive OR and assignment operator	C |= 2 is same as C = C | 2

The following simple example program demonstrates the assignment operators.

```
public class Test {
  public static void main(String args[]) {
    int a = 10;
    int b = 20;
    int c = 0;
    c = a + b;
    System.out.println("c = a + b = " + c );
    c += a ;
    System.out.println("c += a  = " + c );
    c -= a ;
    System.out.println("c -= a = " + c );
    c *= a ;
    System.out.println("c *= a = " + c );
    a = 10;
    c = 15;
    c /= a ;
    System.out.println("c /= a = " + c );
    a = 10;
    c = 15;
    c %= a ;
    System.out.println("c %= a  = " + c );
```

```
    c <<= 2 ;
    System.out.println("c <<= 2 = " + c );
    c >>= 2 ;
    System.out.println("c >>= 2 = " + c );
    c >>= 2 ;
    System.out.println("c >>= a = " + c );
    c &= a ;
    System.out.println("c &= 2  = " + c );
    c ^= a ;
    System.out.println("c ^= a  = " + c );
    c |= a ;
    System.out.println("c |= a  = " + c );
  }
}
```

Misc Operators

There are few other operators supported by Java Language.

Conditional Operator (? :)

Conditional operator is also known as the ternary operator. This operator consists of three operands and is used to evaluate Boolean expressions. The goal of the operator is to decide which value should be assigned to the variable. The operator is written as:

variable x = (expression) ? value if true : value if false

Following is the example:

```
public class Test {
  public static void main(String args[]){
    int a , b;
    a = 10;
    b = (a == 1) ? 20: 30;
    System.out.println( "Value of b is : " +  b );
    b = (a == 10) ? 20: 30;
    System.out.println( "Value of b is : " + b );
  }
}
```

Instance of Operator

This operator is used only for object reference variables. The operator checks whether the object is of a particular type(class type or interface type). Instance of operator is wriiten as:

(Object reference variable) instance of (class/interface type)

If the object referred by the variable on the left side of the operator passes the IS-A check for the class/interface type on the right side, then the result will be true. Following is the

Example

```
public class Test {
  public static void main(String args[]){
    String name = "James";
    // following will return true since name is type of String
    boolean result = name instanceof String;
    System.out.println( result );
  }
}
```

This would produce the following result:

```
true
```

This operator will still return true if the object being compared is the assignment compatible with the type on the right. Following is one more example:

```
class Vehicle {}
public class Car extends Vehicle {
  public static void main(String args[]){
    Vehicle a = new Car();
    boolean result =  a instanceof Car;
    System.out.println( result );
  }
}
```

This would produce the following result:

```
True
```

1.14. Operator Precedence

Precedence of Java Operators

Operator precedence determines the grouping of terms in an expression. This affects how an expression is evaluated. Certain operators have higher precedence than others; for example, the multiplication operator has higher precedence than the addition operator:

For example, x = 7 + 3 * 2; here x is assigned 13, not 20 because operator * has higher precedence than +, so it first gets multiplied with 3*2 and then adds into 7.

Here, operators with the highest precedence appear at the top of the table, those with the lowest appear at the bottom. Within an expression, higher precedence operators will be evaluated first.

Category	Operator	Associativity
Postfix	() [] . (dot operator)	Left to right
Unary	++ - - ! ~	Right to left
Multiplicative	* / %	Left to right
Additive	+ -	Left to right
Shift	>> >>> <<	Left to right
Relational	> >= < <=	Left to right
Equality	== !=	Left to right
Bitwise AND	&	Left to right
Bitwise XOR	^	Left to right
Bitwise OR	|	Left to right
Logical AND	&&	Left to right
Logical OR	||	Left to right
Conditional	?:	Right to left
Assignment	= += -= *= /= %= >>= <<= &= ^= |=	Right to left
Comma	,	Left to right

1.15. Type Casting/Conversion

Assigning a value to one type of variable to another type is called type casting

Java supports two types of castings – **primitive data type casting** and **reference type casting**. Reference type casting is nothing but assigning one Java object to another object. Java data type casting comes with 3 flavors.

- Implicit casting
- Explicit casting
- Boolean casting.

1. *Implicit Casting (Widening Conversion)*

A data type of lower size (occupying less memory) is assigned to a data type of higher size. This is done implicitly by the JVM. The lower size is widened to higher size. This is also named as **automatic type conversion.**

Examples:

```
int x = 10;               // occupies 4 bytes
double y = x;             // occupies 8 bytes
System.out.println(y);    // prints 10.0
```

In the above code 4 bytes integer value is assigned to 8 bytes double value.

2. *Explicit Casting (Narrowing Conversion)*

A data type of higher size (occupying more memory) cannot be assigned to a data type of lower size. This is not done implicitly by the JVM and requires **explicit casting**; a casting operation to be performed by the programmer. The higher size is narrowed to lower size.

```
double x = 10.5;     // 8 bytes
int y = x;           // 4 bytes ; raises compilation error
```

In the above code, 8 bytes double value is narrowed to 4 bytes int value. It raises error. Let us explicitly type cast it.

```
double x = 10.5;
int y = (int) x;
```

The double **x** is explicitly converted to int **y**. The thumb rule is, on both sides, the same data type should exist.

3. *Boolean Casting*

A boolean value cannot be assigned to any other data type. Except boolean, all the remaining 7 data types can be assigned to one another either implicitly or explicitly; but boolean cannot. We say, boolean is **incompatible** for conversion. Maximum we can assign a boolean value to another boolean. Following raises error.

```
boolean x = true;
int y = x;             // error
```

```
boolean x = true;
int y = (int) x;       // error
```

byte -> short -> int -> long -> float -> double. In the above statement, left to right can be assigned implicitly and right to left requires explicit casting. That is, **byte** can be assigned to **short** implicitly but **short** to **byte** requires explicit casting.

Automatic Type Casting Take Place When

- The two types are compatible
- The target type is larger than the source type

Example

```
public class Test
{
  public static void main(String[] args)
  {
   int i = 100;
   long l = i;  //no explicit type casting required
   float f = l;  //no explicit type casting required
   System.out.println("Int value "+i);
   System.out.println("Long value "+l);
   System.out.println("Float value "+f);
  }
}
```

When you are assigning a larger type value to a variable of smaller type, then you need to perform explicit type casting.

Example

```
public class Test
{
  public static void main(String[] args)
  {
   double d = 100.04;
   long l = (long)d;  //explicit type casting required
   int i = (int)l;            //explicit type casting required
   System.out.println("Double value "+d);
   System.out.println("Long value "+l);
   System.out.println("Int value "+i);
  }
}
```

1.16. Statements

There are two types of decision making statements in Java.

They are:

- if statements
- switch statements

The if Statement

An if statement consists of a Boolean expression followed by one or more statements.

Syntax

The syntax of an if statement is:

```
if(Boolean_expression)
{
 //Statements will execute if the Boolean expression is true
}
```

If the Boolean expression evaluates to true then the block of code inside the if statement will be executed. If not the first set of code after the end of the if statement (after the closing curly brace) will be executed.

Example

```
public class Test {
  public static void main(String args[]){
    int x = 10;
    if( x < 20 ){
      System.out.print("This is if statement");
    }
  }
}
```

This would produce the following result: T

his is if statement

The if...else Statement

An if statement can be followed by an optional *else* statement, which executes when the Boolean expression is false.

Syntax

The syntax of an if...else is:

```
if(Boolean_expression)
{
  //Executes when the Boolean expression is true
}else
{
  //Executes when the Boolean expression is false
}
```

Example

```
public class Test {
  public static void main(String args[]){
    int x = 30;
    if( x < 20 )
    {
      System.out.print("This is if statement");
    }else
    {
      System.out.print("This is else statement");
    }
  }
}
```

This would produce the following result:

```
This is else statement
```

The if...else if...else Statement

An if statement can be followed by an optional *else if...else* statement, which is very useful to test various conditions using single if...else if statement. When using if , else if , else statements there are few points to keep in mind.

- An if can have zero or one else's and it must come after any else if's.
- An if can have zero to many else if's and they must come before the else.
- Once an else if succeeds, none of the remaining else if's or else's will be tested.

Syntax

The syntax of an if...else is:

```
if(Boolean_expression 1){
  //Executes when the Boolean expression 1 is true
}else if(Boolean_expression 2){
  //Executes when the Boolean expression 2 is true
}else if(Boolean_expression 3){
  //Executes when the Boolean expression 3 is true
}else {
  //Executes when the none of the above condition is true.
}
```

Example

```
public class Test {
  public static void main(String args[]){
    int x = 30;
    if( x == 10 ){
      System.out.print("Value of X is 10");
    }else if( x == 20 ){
      System.out.print("Value of X is 20");
    }else if( x == 30 ){
      System.out.print("Value of X is 30");
    }else{
      System.out.print("This is else statement");
    }
  }
}
```

This would produce the following result:

```
Value of X is 30
```

Nested if...else Statement

It is always legal to nest if-else statements which means you can use one if or else if statement inside another if or else if statement.

Syntax

The syntax for a nested if...else is as follows:

```
if(Boolean_expression 1){
  //Executes when the Boolean expression 1 is true
  if(Boolean_expression 2){
    //Executes when the Boolean expression 2 is true
  }
}
```

You can nest *else if...else* in the similar way as we have nested *if* statement.

Example

```
public class Test {
  public static void main(String args[]){
    int x = 30;
    int y = 10;
    if( x == 30 ){
      if( y == 10 ){
        System.out.print("X = 30 and Y = 10");
      }
    }
  }
}
```

This would produce the following result: X = 30 and Y = 10

The switch Statement

A *switch* statement allows a variable to be tested for equality against a list of values. Each value is called a case, and the variable being switched on is checked for each case.

Syntax

The syntax of enhanced for loop is:

```
switch(expression){
  case value :
    //Statements
    break; //optional
  case value :
```

```
        //Statements
        break; //optional
    //You can have any number of case statements.
    default : //Optional
        //Statements
}
```

The following rules apply to a switch statement:

- The variable used in a switch statement can only be a byte, short, int, or char.
- You can have any number of case statements within a switch. Each case is followed by the value to be compared to and a colon.
- The value for a case must be the same data type as the variable in the switch and it must be a constant or a literal.
- When the variable being switched on is equal to a case, the statements following that case will execute until a break statement is reached.
- When a break statement is reached, the switch terminates, and the flow of control jumps to the next line following the switch statement.
- Not every case needs to contain a break. If no break appears, the flow of control will fall through to subsequent cases until a break is reached.
- A switch statement can have an optional default case, which must appear at the end of the switch. The default case can be used for performing a task when none of the cases is true. No break is needed in the default case.

Example

```
public class Test {
  public static void main(String args[]){
    //char grade = args[0].charAt(0);
    char grade = 'C';
    switch(grade)
    {
      case 'A' :
        System.out.println("Excellent!");
     break;
      case 'B' :
      case 'C' :
```

```
            System.out.println("Well done");
            break;
         case 'D' :
            System.out.println("You passed");
         case 'F' :
            System.out.println("Better try again");
            break;
         default :
            System.out.println("Invalid grade");
      }
      System.out.println("Your grade is " + grade);
   }
}
```

There may be a situation when we need to execute a block of code several number of times, and is often referred to as a loop. Java has very flexible three looping mechanisms. You can use one of the following three loops:

- while Loop
- do...while Loop
- for Loop

As of Java 5, the *enhanced for loop* was introduced. This is mainly used for Arrays.

The while Loop

A while loop is a control structure that allows you to repeat a task a certain number of times.

Syntax

The syntax of a while loop is:

```
while(Boolean_expression)
{
  //Statements
}
```

When executing, if the *boolean_expression* result is true, then the actions inside the loop will be executed. This will continue as long as the expression result is true. Here, key point of the *while* loop is that the loop might not ever run. When the expression is tested and the result is false, the loop body will be skipped and the first statement after the while loop will be executed.

Example

```
public class Test {
  public static void main(String args[]) {
    int x = 10;
    while( x < 20 ) {
      System.out.print("value of x : " + x );
      x++;
      System.out.print("\n");
    }
  }
}
```

This would produce the following result:

```
value of x : 10
value of x : 11
value of x : 12
value of x : 13
value of x : 14
value of x : 15
value of x : 16
value of x : 17
value of x : 18
value of x : 19
```

The do...while Loop

A do...while loop is similar to a while loop, except that a do...while loop is guaranteed to execute at least one time.

Syntax

The syntax of a do...while loop is:

```
do
{
  //Statements
} while(Boolean_expression);
```

Notice that the Boolean expression appears at the end of the loop, so the statements in the loop execute once before the Boolean is tested.

If the Boolean expression is true, the flow of control jumps back up to do, and the statements in the loop execute again. This process repeats until the Boolean expression is false.

Example

```
public class Test {
  public static void main(String args[]){
    int x = 10;
    do{
      System.out.print("value of x : " + x );
      x++;
      System.out.print("\n");
    }while( x < 20 );
  }
}
```

This would produce the following result:

```
value of x : 10
value of x : 11
value of x : 12
value of x : 13
value of x : 14
value of x : 15
value of x : 16
value of x : 17
value of x : 18
value of x : 19
```

The for Loop

A for loop is a repetition control structure that allows you to efficiently write a loop that needs to execute a specific number of times.

A for loop is useful when you know how many times a task is to be repeated.

Syntax

The syntax of a for loop is:

```
for(initialization; Boolean_expression; update)
{
  //Statements
}
```

Here is the flow of control in a for loop:

- The initialization step is executed first, and only once. This step allows you to declare and initialize any loop control variables. You are not required to put a statement here, as long as a semicolon appears.
- Next, the Boolean expression is evaluated. If it is true, the body of the loop is executed. If it is false, the body of the loop does not execute and flow of control jumps to the next statement past the for loop.
- After the body of the for loop executes, the flow of control jumps back up to the update statement. This statement allows you to update any loop control variables. This statement can be left blank, as long as a semicolon appears after the Boolean expression.
- The Boolean expression is now evaluated again. If it is true, the loop executes and the process repeats itself (body of loop, then update step, then Boolean expression). After the Boolean expression is false, the for loop terminates.

Example

```
public class Test {
  public static void main(String args[]) {
    for(int x = 10; x < 20; x = x+1) {
      System.out.print("value of x : " + x );
      System.out.print("\n");
    }
  }
}
```

This would produce the following result:

```
value of x : 10
value of x : 11
value of x : 12
```

```
value of x : 13
value of x : 14
value of x : 15
value of x : 16
value of x : 17
value of x : 18
value of x : 19
```

Enhanced for Loop in Java

As of Java 5, the enhanced for loop was introduced. This is mainly used for Arrays.

Syntax

The syntax of enhanced for loop is:

```
for(declaration : expression)
{
  //Statements
}
```

- **Declaration:** The newly declared block variable, which is of a type compatible with the elements of the array you are accessing. The variable will be available within the for block and its value would be the same as the current array element.
- **Expression:** This evaluates to the array you need to loop through. The expression can be an array variable or method call that returns an array.

Example

```
public class Test {
  public static void main(String args[]){
    int [] numbers = {10, 20, 30, 40, 50};
    for(int x : numbers ){
      System.out.print( x );
      System.out.print(",");
    }
    System.out.print("\n");
    String [] names ={"James", "Larry", "Tom", "Lacy"};
    for( String name : names ) {
      System.out.print( name );
```

```
      System.out.print(",");
    }
  }
}
```

This would produce the following result:

10, 20,30,40,50

James, Larry, Tom, Lacy,

The Break Keyword

The break keyword is used to stop the entire loop. The break keyword must be used inside any loop or a switch statement.

The break keyword will stop the execution of the innermost loop and start executing the next line of code after the block.

Syntax

The syntax of a break is a single statement inside any loop:

```
break;
```

Example

```
public class Test {
  public static void main(String args[]) {
    int [] numbers = {10, 20, 30, 40, 50};
    for(int x : numbers ) {
      if( x == 30 ) {
            break;
      }
      System.out.print( x );
      System.out.print("\n");
    }
  }
}
```

This would produce the following result:

10

20

The Continue Keyword

The *continue* keyword can be used in any of the loop control structures. It causes the loop to immediately jump to the next iteration of the loop.

- In a for loop, the continue keyword causes flow of control to immediately jump to the update statement.
- In a while loop or do/while loop, flow of control immediately jumps to the Boolean expression.

Syntax

The syntax of a continue is a single statement inside any loop:

```
continue;
```

Example

```
public class Test {
  public static void main(String args[]) {
    int [] numbers = {10, 20, 30, 40, 50};
    for(int x : numbers ) {
      if( x == 30 ) {
            continue;
      }
      System.out.print( x );
      System.out.print("\n");
    }
  }
}
```

This would produce the following result:

```
10
20
40
50
```

1.17. Summary

OOP is a new way of organizing and developing programs. It eliminates many pitfalls of the conventional programming approach. OOP programs are organized around objects, which contain data and functions that operate on that data. A class is a template for a number of objects. The object is an instance of a class. The major features of OOP are data abstraction, data encapsulation, inheritance and polymorphism. This new methodology increases programmer productivity, delivers better quality of software and lessens maintenance cost. Languages that support several OOP concepts include C++, Smalltalk, Object Pascal and Java.

1.18. Questions

1. Briefly Explain any six key consideration used for designing JAVA Language?
2. Discusses three Oops Principles
3. How compile once and run anywhere is implemented in JAVA?
4. List down various operators available in JAVA Language?
5. List and Explain java Buzz words
6. Explain different aces specifiers in Java with Examples?
7. **I).** int num ,den;

   ```
   if (den!=0 &&num|den>2)
     {
     }
   ```

   ii. int num ,den;

   ```
   if (den!=0 &&num|den = =2)
     {
     }
   ```

   Compare and explain the above snippet code.
8. Write a note on object instaniation?
9. What is polymorphism explain with an Example?
10. Explain the process of building and running a java application?
11. Explain the following i). JVM ii). Type casting.
12.
   ```
   class example{
   public static void main(string s[]) {
   int a
   for(a=0;a<3;a++){
   int b=-1;
   System.out.println("  "+ b);
   b=50;
   System.out.println("      "+b);
   }}
   }
   ```

What is the output of the above code? If you insert another "**int b**" outside the for loop, what is the ouput?

13. With example explain the working of >> and >>>.
14. What is the default package and default class in Java?
15. Write a program to calculate the average among the elements {4, 5, 7, 8} using for each in Java. How for each is different from for loop?
16. How arrays defined and used in Java?
17. Discuss the labeled break and continue statements?
18. Briefly discuss about the java development tool kit.

UNIT-2

CLASSES, INHERITANCE, EXCEPTIONS, APPLET

2.1. Objectives

After Going Through this Unit, you should be Able to

- Define class, declare class and understand what class is composed of.
- Understand what is constructor, overload constructor, override constructor.
- Explain the uses of super keyword, this keyword.
- Create the instance of class and access members of class through objects.
- Explain the different types of inheritance.
- Explain the different types of Exceptions in Java and also able to handle different types of exceptions in the programs.
- Understand applet, explain the applet architecture.
- Design small application in java using applet.
- Describe Java Applets and its Importance;
- Explain Applet architecture;
- Compile and Execute Java Applet programs;
- Use Event Handling constructs of Java programs, and
- Apply various HTML tags to execute the Applet programs.

2.2. Classes in Java

In Java a class is a template for an object, and an object is an *instance* of a class. Because an object is an instance of a class.

When you define a class, you declare its exact form and nature. Since Java is an object oriented language, complete java language is build on classes and object. Java is also known as a strong **Object oriented programming language** (oops).

2.3. Declaring a Class

A class is declared using **class** keyword. A class contains both data and code that operate on that data.

The data or variables defined within a **class** are called **instance variables** and the code that operates on this data is known as **methods**.

A simplified general form of a **class** definition is shown here:

```
class classname {
type instance-variable1;
type instance-variable2;
// ...
type instance-variableN;
type methodname1(parameter-list) {
// body of method
}
type methodname2(parameter-list) {
// body of method
}
// ...
type methodnameN(parameter-list) {
// body of method
}
}
```

Rules for Java Class

- A class can have only public or default (no modifier) access specifier.
- It can be either abstract, final or concrete (normal class).
- It must have the class keyword, and class must be followed by a legal identifier.
- It may optionally extend one parent class. By default, it will extend java.lang.Object.
- It may optionally implement any number of comma-separated interfaces.
- The class's variables and methods are declared within a set of curly braces {}.
- Each **.java** source file may contain only one public class. A source file may contain any number of default visible classes.
- Finally, the source file name must match the public class name and it must have a .java suffix.

2.4. Class Name

Class name should be defined after the keyword class. Here is a class called **Box** that defines three instance variables: **width**, **height**, and **depth**. Currently, **Box** does not contain any methods.

```
class Box {
double width;
double height;
double depth;
}
```

Methods in Java

Method describe behavior of an object. A method is a collection of statements that are group together to perform an operation.

Syntax

```
return-type methodName(parameter-list)
{
//body of method
}
```

Example of a Method

```
public String getName(String st)
{
 String name="StudyTonight";
 name=name+st;
 return name;
}
```

2.5. Constructors

Constructor is a member function whose name is same as that of class. Java allows objects to initialize themselves when they are created. This automatic initialization is performed through the use of a constructor. A constructor initializes an object immediately upon creation. Once defined, the constructor is automatically called immediately after the object is created, before the new operator completes.

- Constructors don't have return type, not even **void**.
- The implicit return type of a class' constructor is the class type itself.

2.6. Super Classes

A superclass is a class that has been extended by another class. It allows the extending class to inherit its state and behaviors.

Also Known As: base class, parent class

Imagine you define a Person class:

```
public class Person
{

}
```

A new class can be created by extending this class:

```
public class Employee extends Person
{

}
```

The Person class is said to be the superclass of the Employee class. Super has two general forms or super has two uses.

- The first calls the superclass' constructor.
- The second is used to access a member of the superclass that has been hidden by a member of a subclass.

Using Super to Call Superclass Constructors

A subclass can call a constructor defined by its super class by use of the following form of

super(arg-list);

Here, arg-list specifies any arguments needed by the constructor in the superclass. super ( ) must always be the first statement executed inside a subclass' constructor.

To see how **super( )** is used, consider this improved version of the **BoxWeight( )** class:

```
// BoxWeight now uses super to initialize its Box attributes.
class BoxWeight extends Box
{
double weight; // weight of box
// initialize width, height, and depth using super()
BoxWeight(double w, double h, double d, double m) {
super(w, h, d); // call superclass constructor
weight = m;
}
}
```

A Second Use for Super

The second form of **super** acts somewhat like **this**, except that it always refers to the superclass of the subclass in which it is used. This usage has the following general form:

super. member

Here, member can be either a method or an instance variable. This second form of **super** is most applicable to situations in which member names of a subclass hide members by the same name in the superclass.

Consider this simple class hierarchy:

```
// Using super to overcome name hiding.
class A {
int i;
}
// Create a subclass by extending class A.
class B extends A {
int i; // this i hides the i in A
B(int a, int b) {
super.i = a; // i in A
i = b; // i in B
}
void show() {
System.out.println("i in superclass: " + super.i);
System.out.println("i in subclass: " + i);
}
}
class UseSuper {
public static void main(String args[]) {
B subOb = new B(1, 2);
subOb.show();
}
}
```

This program displays the following:

i in superclass: 1

i in subclass: 2

Although the instance variable **i** in **B** hides the **i** in **A**, **super** allows access to the **i** defined in the superclass. As we will see, **super** can also be used to call methods that are hidden by a subclass.

2.7. Constructors

Constructor is a special member function who's name is same as the name of the class . Constructor's syntax does not include a return type, since constructors never return a value.

Constructors may include parameters of various types. When the constructor is invoked using the new operator, the types must match those that are specified in the constructor definition.

Java provides a default constructor which takes no arguments and performs no special actions or initializations, when no explicit constructors are provided.

The only action taken by the implicit default constructor is to call the superclass constructor using the super() call. Constructor arguments provide you with a way to provide parameters for the initialization of an object.

Example:

```
public class Cube1 {
        int length;
        int breadth;
        int height;
        public int getVolume() {
                return (length * breadth * height);
        }
        Cube1() {
                length = 10;
                breadth = 10;
                height = 10;
        }
        Cube1(int l, int b, int h) {
                length = l;
                breadth = b;
                height = h;
        }
```

```
    public static void main(String[] args) {
            Cube1 cubeObj1, cubeObj2;
            cubeObj1 = new Cube1();
            cubeObj2 = new Cube1(10, 20, 30);
System.out.println("Volume of Cube1 is : " +         cubeObj1.getVolume());
System.out.println("Volume of Cube1 is : " + cubeObj2.getVolume());
    }
}
```

Constructors are similar to methods, but with some important differences.

- **Constructor name is class name**. A constructors must have the same name as the class it's in.
- **Default constructor**. If you don't define a constructor for a class, a default parameterless constructor is automatically created by the compiler. The default constructor calls the default parent constructor (super()) and initializes all instance variables to default value (zero for numeric types, null for object references, and false for booleans).
- **Default constructor is created only if there are no constructors**. If you define any constructor for your class, no default constructor is automatically created.

Differences between Methods and Constructors

- There is *no return type* given in a constructor signature (header). The value is this object itself so there is no need to indicate a return value.
- There is *no return statement* in the body of the constructor.
- The *first line* of a constructor must either be a call on another constructor in the same class (using this), or a call on the superclass constructor (using super). If the first line is neither of these, the compiler automatically inserts a call to the parameterless super class constructor.
- **this(...) - Calls another constructor in same class**. Often a constructor with few parameters will call a constructor with more parameters, giving default values for the missing parameters. Use *this to call other constructors* in the same class.
- **super(...)**. Use *super* to call a constructor in a parent class. Calling the constructor for the superclass must be the *first statement* in the body of a constructor. If you are satisfied with the default constructor in the superclass, there is no need to make a call to it because it will be supplied automatically.

Default Constructor – No Argument Constructor: A constructor without parameters is called as "**default constructor**" or "**no-args constructor**".

It is called default because if the programmer does not write himself, JVM creates one and supplies. The default constructor supplied by the JVM does not have any functionality (output).

Constructor Overloading

Just like method overloading, constructors also can be overloaded. Same constructor declared with different parameters in the same class is known as constructor overloading. Compiler differentiates which constructor is to be called depending upon the number of parameters and their sequence of data types.

Example

```
public class Perimeter
{
 public Perimeter()          // I constructor
 {
  System.out.println("From default");
 }
 public Perimeter(int x)   // II constructor
 {
  System.out.println("Circle perimeter: " + 2*Math.PI*x);
 }
 public Perimeter(int x, int y) // III constructor
 {
  System.out.println("Rectangle perimeter: " +2*(x+y));
 }
 public static void main(String args[])
 {
  Perimeter p1 = new Perimeter();     // I constructor called
  Perimeter p2 = new Perimeter(10);  // II constructor called
  Perimeter p3 = new Perimeter(10, 20); // III constructor called
 }
}
```

Java Constructors: Using super() statement:

```
class Animal
{
 public Animal()                    // I
 {
  System.out.println("All animals eat");
 }
 public Animal(String name1)        // II
 {
  System.out.println("Animal name is " + name1);
 }
}
public class Lion extends Animal
{
 public Lion()                      // III
 {
  System.out.println("Lion eats other animals");
 }
 public Lion(String name1)          // IV
 {
  super("Bushy Animal");
  System.out.println("Lion name is " + name1);
 }
 public static void main(String args[])
 {
  Lion l1 = new Lion("King");       // calls IV
 }
}
```

Order of Constructor Calling in Multilevel Inheritance

When the object of a subclass is created the constructor of the subclass is called which in turn calls constructor of its immediate superclass. For example, if we take a case of multilevel inheritance, where class B inherits from class A. and class C inherits from class B. You can see the output of the example program given below, which show the order of constructor calling.

```
// Program
Class A
{
A()
{
System.out.println("Constructor of Class A has been called");
}
}
class B extends A
{
B()
{
super();
System.out.println("Constructor of Class B has been called");
}
}
class C extends B
{
C()
{
super();
System.out.println("Constructor of Class C has been called");
}}
class Constructor_Call
{
public static void main(String[] args)
{
System.out.println("------Welcome to Constructor call Demo------"); C objc = new C();
}
}
```

Output

------Welcome to Constructor call Demo------
Constructor of Class A has been called
Constructor of Class B has been called
Constructor of Class C has been called

2.8. Creating Instances of Class

In Java instance of the class can be created using the keyword **new.** Example assume that you have the class called **Box** then the instance of the class Box can be created as shown below:

Box b = new Box(); // b is the instance of the class Box

2.9. Inner Classes

A class written inside another class is known as **"inner class" or "nested class"**. That is, an inner class is enclosed within another class. Inner classes give more **accessibility and scope restrictions** for other classes.

Types of Inner Classes

There are four styles of creating an inner class.

- Static member classes
- Member classes
- Local classes
- Anonymous classes

Static Member Classes

Here, the inner class is declared as **static**. Static inner classes are less used. Following program illustrates.t5r

```
public class First
{
 static class Second
 {
  public static void area(int x)
  {
   System.out.println("Area is " + (Math.round(3.14*x*x)));
  }
 }
 public static void main(String args[] )
 {
  FirstOne.SecondOne.area(10);
 }
}
```

Member Classes

Here, the inner class is not declared as static. It is declared within the body of the outer class (not inside the method of outer class). Following are the **scope rules.**

- The outer class members (variables) can be accessed by inner class.
- The inner class members cannot be accessed by outer class.
- Inner class members can be accessed by inner class only.

Following program illustrates the above scope rules.

```
public class First   // Top-level class; outer class or enclosing class
{
 int price = 100;  // variable of outer class
 class Second      // inner class as a member of outer class
 {
  int rate = 200;           // variable of inner class
  public void display()     // inner class method
  {
   System.out.println("price from display() method: " + price);
   System.out.println("rate from display method: " + rate );
  }
 }                   // inner class closes
 public void show()         // outer class method
 {
  System.out.println("pirce from show() method: " + price);
  // System.out.println("y from outer method: " + y);  // raises compilation error, scope
problem
 }
 public static void main(String args[])
 {
  First f1 = new First();
  First.Second fs = new First( ).new Second();
  f1.show();
  fs.display();
 }
}
```

Local Classes

A **local class** is simply an inner class but declared within the method of outer class (earlier, the inner class exists directly in the body of the outer class but now exists inside a method). Here the rules of accessibility are, **the inner class can access, anyhow, its own members and only the final parameters of the enclosing method.**

Following program illustrates.

```
public class Father
{
 double price = 10.5;        // outer class field (variable)
 public void area(int x , final int y)  // outer class method
 {
  int k = x + y;      // non-final variable of outer class
  final int m = x * y; // final variable of outer class
  class Son   // inner class inside the method area() of outer class
  {
   public void perimeter()
   {
 // System.out.println("x is " + x); // error as x non-final
  System.out.println("y is " + y);   // no error as y is final
 //System.out.println("k is " + k);  // error as k is non-final
  System.out.println("m is " + m);    // no error as m is final
  System.out.println("price  is " + price);
   }// price is not final, but works as it is a field (not parameter)
  }  // inner class closes
  Son s1 = new Son();
  s1.perimeter();
 } // outer method closes
 public static void main(String args[])
 {
  Father f1 = new Father();
  f1.area(10, 20);
 }
}
```

Anonymous Inner Class

An anonymous inner class, as the name indicates, does not have a name. As it does not contain a name, it must be instantiated at the time of defining it. This type of anonymous classes is mostly used in event handling mechanism of AWT. Following snippet of code is used to close the frame window.

```
addWindowListener( new WindowAdapter()
    {
            public void windowClosing(WindowEvent e)
        {
                    Sytem.exit( 0 ) ;
            }
        }
    ) ;
```

2.10. Inheritance: Simple, Multiple, and Multilevel Inheritance

Types of Inheritance

- Single inheritance
- Multilevel inheritance
- Multiple inheritance
- Hierarchical inheritance
    - In **single inheritance**, one class extends one class only.
    - In **multilevel inheritance**, the ladder of single inheritance increases.
    - In **multiple inheritance**, one class directly extends more than one class.
    - In **hierarchical inheritance** one class is extended by more than one class.

Multilevel Inheritance: In multilevel, one-to-one ladder increases. Multiple classes are involved in inheritance, but one class extends only one. The lowermost subclass can make use of all its super classes' members. Multilevel inheritance is an indirect way of implementing multiple inheritance.

2.11. Overriding, Overloading

Method Overloading: Method overloading is the process of defining two or more methods within the same class that share the same name, as long as their parameter declarations are different. Method overloading is one of the ways that Java supports polymorphism.

- When an overloaded method is invoked, Java uses the type and/or number of arguments as its guide to determine which version of the overloaded method to actually call.

- The, overloaded methods must differ in the type and/or number of their parameters.
- While overloaded methods may have different return types, the return type alone is insufficient to distinguish two versions of a method.
- When Java encounters a call to an overloaded method, it simply executes the version of the method whose parameters match the arguments used in the call.

```
// Demonstrate method overloading.
 class OverloadDemo
 {
 void add()
 {
System.out.println("No parameters");
 }
//Overload test for one integer parameter.
 void add(int a)
 {
  a= a+a;
System.out.println("a: " + a);
}
Overload test for two integer parameters.
 void add(int a, int b)
 {
System.out.println("Addition of a and b: " +(a+b) );
 }
overload test for a double parameter
    double add(double a)
{
 System.out.println("double a: " + a); return a*a;
}
}
class Overload {
public static void main(String args[])
{
 OverloadDemo ob = new OverloadDemo(); double result;
// call all versions of test() ob.test();
```

```
ob.add(10); ob.(10, 20);
result = ob.add(123.25);
System.out.println("Result of ob.add(123.25): " + result);
}
}
```

Method Overriding: The method is said to be overridden if the method is defined in subclass also with same name, return type and number of arguments

The following program creates a superclass called Figure that stores the dimensions of a two-dimensional object. It also defines a method called area( ) that computes the area of an object. The program derives two subclasses from Figure. The first is Rectangle and the second is Triangle. Each of these subclasses overrides area( ) so that it returns the area of a rectangle and a triangle, respectively.

```
// Using run-time polymorphism. class Figure {
double dim1; double dim2;
Figure(double a, double b) { dim1 = a;
dim2 = b;
}
double area() {
System.out.println("Area for Figure is undefined."); return 0;
}
}
class Rectangle extends Figure { Rectangle(double a, double b) {
super(a, b);
}
// override area for rectangle double area() {
System.out.println("Inside Area for Rectangle."); return dim1 * dim2;
}
}
class Triangle extends Figure { Triangle(double a, double b) {
super(a, b);
}
// override area for right triangle double area() {
System.out.println("Inside Area for Triangle."); return dim1 * dim2 / 2;
}
```

```
}
class FindAreas {
public static void main(String args[]) { Figure f = new Figure(10, 10); Rectangle r = new
Rectangle(9, 5); Triangle t = new Triangle(10, 8);
Figure figref;
figref = r;
System.out.println("Area is " + figref.area());
figref = t;
System.out.println("Area is " + figref.area());
figref = f;
System.out.println("Area is " + figref.area());
}
}
```

2.12. Exception Handling

A Java exception is an object that describes an exceptional (that is, error) condition that has occurred in a piece of code. When an exceptional condition arises, an object representing that exception is created and *thrown* in the method that caused the error. Exceptions can be generated by the Java run-time system, or they can be manually generated by your code.

Java exception handling is managed via five keywords: **try**, **catch**, **throw**, **throws**, and **finally**.

This is the general form of an exception-handling block:

```
try {
// block of code to monitor for errors
}
catch (ExceptionType1 exOb) {
// exception handler for ExceptionType1
}
catch (ExceptionType2 exOb) {
// exception handler for ExceptionType2
}
// ...
finally {
// block of code to be executed after try block ends}
```

Exception Types

All exception types are subclasses of the built-in class **Throwable**. Thus, **Throwable** is super class for all other subclass of exception classes. **Throwable** have two subclasses **Exception and Error**. Exception class is used for exceptional conditions that user programs should catch. This is also the class that you will subclass to create your own custom exception types. There is an important subclass of **Exception**, called **RuntimeException**. Exceptions of this type are automatically defined for the programs that you write and include things such as division by zero and invalid array indexing. **Error**, defines exceptions that are not expected to be caught under normal circumstances by your program. Exceptions of type **Error** are used by the Java run-time system to indicate errors having to do with the run-time environment, itself. Stack overflow is an example of such an error. Uncaught Exceptions: Before learning how to handle exceptions in our program, it is useful to see what happens when we don't handle them. This small program includes an expression that intentionally causes a divide-by-zero error:

```
class Exc0 {
public static void main(String args[]) { int d = 0;
int a = 42 / d;
}
}
```

When the Java run-time system detects the attempt to divide by zero, it constructs a new exception object and then *throws* this exception. This causes the execution of **Exc0** to stop, because once an exception has been thrown, it must be *caught* by an exception handler and dealt with immediately. Here we are not handling the exception manually Therefore the exception is caught by the default handler provided by the Java run-time system. Any exception that is not caught by our program will ultimately be processed by the default handler. The default handler displays a string describing the exception, prints a stack trace from the point at which the exception occurred, and terminates the program. Here is the exception generated when this example is executed:

```
java.lang.ArithmeticException: / by zero at Exc0.main(Exc0.java:4)
```

Using try and catch: Although the default exception handler provided by the Java run-time system is useful for debugging. Sometimes we want to handle an exception ourself. Doing so provides two benefits. First, it allows us to fix the error. Second, it prevents the program from automatically terminating. To guard against and handle a run-time error, simply enclose the code that you want to monitor inside a try block. Immediately following the try block, include a catch clause that specifies the exception type that you wish to catch. The following program includes a try block and a catch clause that processes the ArithmeticException generated by the division-by-zero error:

```
class Exc2 {
public static void main(String args[]) { int d, a;
try { // monitor a block of code. d = 0;
a = 42 / d;
System.out.println("This will not be printed.");
} catch (ArithmeticException e) { // catch divide-by-zero error System.out.println("Division
by zero.");
}
System.out.println("After catch statement.");
}
}
```

This program generates the following output:

Division by zero.

After catch statement.

Multiple catch Clauses: In some cases, more than one exception could be raised by a single piece of code. To handle this type of situation, you can specify two or more catch clauses, each catching a different type of exception. When an exception is thrown, each catch statement is inspected in order, and the first one whose type matches that of the exception is executed. After one catch statement executes, the others are bypassed, and execution continues after the try/catch block. The following example traps two different exception types:

```
// Demonstrate multiple catch statements. class MultiCatch {
public static void main(String args[]) { try {
int a = args.length; System.out.println("a = " + a); int b = 42 / a;
int c[] = { 1 }; c[42] = 99;
} catch(ArithmeticException e) { System.out.println("Divide by 0: " + e);
} catch(ArrayIndexOutOfBoundsException e) {
System.out.println("Array index oob: " + e);
}
System.out.println("After try/catch blocks.");
}
}
```

This program will cause a division-by-zero exception if it is started with no command-line arguments, since **a** will equal zero. It will survive the division if you provide a command-line argument, setting **a**to something larger than zero.

But it will cause an ArrayIndexOutOfBoundsException, since the **int** array **c** has a length of 1, yet the program attempts to assign a value to **c[42]**.

Here is the output generated by running it both ways:

```
C:\>java MultiCatch a = 0
Divide by 0: java.lang.ArithmeticException: / by zero After try/catch blocks.
C:\>java MultiCatch TestArg a = 1
Array index oob: java.lang.ArrayIndexOutOfBoundsException:42 After try/catch blocks.
```

Nested try Statements: a try statement inside another try is called Nested try . Each time a try statement is entered, the context of that exception is pushed on the stack. If an inner try statement does not have a catch handler for a particular exception, the stack is unwound and the next try statement's catch handlers are inspected for a match. This continues until one of the catch statements succeeds, or until all of the nested try statements are exhausted. If no catch statement matches, then the Java run-time system will handle the exception. Here is an example that uses nested try statements:

```
// An example of nested try statements. class NestTry {
public static void main(String args[]) { try {
int a = args.length;
/*              If no command-line args are present, the following statement will generate a
divide-by-zero exception. */
int b = 42 / a;
System.out.println("a = " + a);
try { // nested try block
/*              If one command-line arg is used, then a divide-by-zero exception
will be generated by the following code. */ if(a==1) a = a/(a-a); // division by zero
/* If two command-line args are used,
then generate an out-of-bounds exception. */ if(a==2) {
int c[] = { 1 };
c[42] = 99; // generate an out-of-bounds exception
}
} catch(ArrayIndexOutOfBoundsException e) { System.out.println("Array index out-of-
bounds: " + e);
```

```
}
} catch(ArithmeticException e) { System.out.println("Divide by 0: " + e);
}
}
}
```

2.13. The Applet Class

Java is an Object Oriented Programming language, supported by various classes. The Applet class is packed in the *Java.* Applet package which has several interfaces. These interfaces enable the creation of Applets, interaction of Applets with the browser, and playing audio clips in Applets. In Java 2, class Javax.swing.Apple is used to define an Applet that uses the Swing GUI components.

As you know, in Java class hierarchy Object is the base class of Java.lang package.

The Applet is placed into the hierarchy as follows:

Java.lang.Object
↓
Java.awt.Component
↓
Java.awt.Container
↓
Java.awt.Panel
↓
Java.applet.Applet

Now let us see what you should do using Java Applet and what you should not do using it.

Below is the list given for Do's and Don'ts of Java Applets:

Do's

- Draw pictures on a web page
- Create a new window and draw the picture in it.
- Play sounds.
- Receive input from the user through the keyboard or the mouse.
- Make a network connection to the server from where the Applet is downloaded,
- and send to and receive arbitrary data from that server.

Don'ts

- Write data on any of the host's disks.
- Read any data from the host's disks without the user's permission. In some environments.

- Notably Netscape, an Applet cannot read data from the user's disks even with permission.
- Delete files
- Read from or write to arbitrary blocks of memory, even on a non-memory-protected operating system like the MacOS
- Make a network connection to a host on the Internet other than the one from which it was downloaded.
- Call the native API directly (though Java API calls may eventually lead back to native API calls).
- Introduce a virus or Trojan horse into the host system.

2.14. Two Types of Applets

At the outset there are two varieties of applets.

- The first are those based directly on the **Applet** class. These applets use the Abstract Window Toolkit (AWT) to provide the graphic user interface (or use no GUI at all). This style of applet has been available since Java was first created.
- The second types of applets are those based on the Swing class **JApplet**. Swing applets use the Swing classes to provide the GUI. Swing offers a richer and often easier-to-use user interface than does the AWT. Thus, Swing-based applets are now the most popular. However, traditional AWT-based applets are still used.

Since **JApplet** inherits **Applet**, all the features of **Applet** are also available in **JApplet**, and most of the information applies to both types of applets.

2.15. Applet Basics

All applets are subclasses (either directly or indirectly) of **Applet**. Applets are not stand-alone programs. Instead, they run within either a web browser or an applet viewer. The illustrations shown in this chapter were created with the standard applet viewer, called **appletviewer**, provided by the JDK. But you can use any applet viewer or browser you like.

Execution of an applet does not begin at **main( )**. Actually, few applets even have **main( )** methods. Instead, execution of an applet is started and controlled with an entirely different mechanism, Output to your applet's window is not performed by **System.out.println( )**. Rather, in non-Swing applets, output is handled with various AWT methods, such as **drawString( )**, which outputs a string to a specified X,Y location. Input is also handled differently than in a console application. (Remember, Swing-based applets use the Swing classes to handle user interactions, and they are described later in this book.)

To use an applet, it is specified in an HTML file. One way to do this is by using the APPLET tag. (The OBJECT tag can also be used, but Sun currently recommends the APPLET tag and this is the tag used by examples in this book.) The applet will be executed by a Java-enabled web browser when it encounters the APPLET tag within the HTML file. To view and test an applet more conveniently, simply include a comment at the head of your Java source code file that contains the APPLET tag. This way, your code is documented with the necessary HTML statements needed by your applet, and you can test the compiled applet by starting the applet viewer with your Java source code file specified as the target. Here is an example of such a comment:

```
/*
<applet code="MyApplet" width=200 height=60> </applet>
*/
```

This comment contains an APPLET tag that will run an applet called **MyApplet** in a window that is 200 pixels wide and 60 pixels high. Because the inclusion of an APPLET command makes testing applets easier, all of the applets shown in this book will contain the appropriate APPLET tag embedded in a comment.

The Applet Class

The **Applet** class defines the methods. **Applet** provides all necessary support for applet execution, such as starting and stopping. It also provides methods that load and display images, and methods that load and play audio clips. **Applet** extends the AWT class **Panel**. In turn, **Panel** extends **Container**, which extends **Component**. These classes provide support for Java's window-based, graphical interface. Thus, **Applet** provides all of the necessary support for window-based activities.

2.16. Applet Architecture

Java Applets are essentially Java programs that run within a web page. Applet programs are Java classes that extend the Java.Applet.Applet class and are embedded by reference within a HTML page. You can observe that when Applets are combined with HTML, they can make an interface more dynamic and powerful than with HTML alone. While some Applets do nothing more than scroll text or play animations, but by incorporating these basic features in web pages you can make them dynamic. These dynamic web pages can be used in an enterprise application to view or manipulate data coming from some source on the server. For example, an Applet may be used to browse and modify records in a database or control runtime aspects of some other application running on the server.

Besides the class file defining the Java Applet itself, Applets can use a collection of utility classes, either by themselves or archived into a JAR file. The Applets and their class files are distributed through standard HTTP requests and therefore can be sent across firewalls with the web page data. Applet code is refreshed automatically each time the user revisits the hosting web site. Therefore, keeps full application up to date on each client desktop on which it is running.

Since Applets are extensions of the Java platform, you can reuse existing Java components when you build web application interface with Applets. As we'll see in example programs in this unit, we can use complex Java objects developed originally for server-side applications as components of your Applets. In fact, you can write Java code that can operate as either an Applet or an application.

In Figure below, you can see that using Applet program running in a Java-enabled web browser you can communicate to the server.

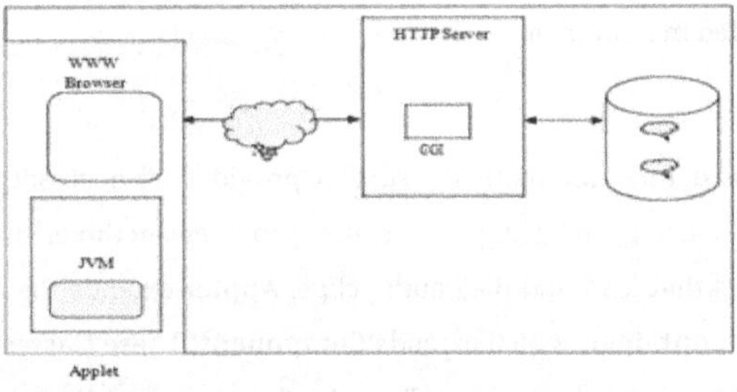

Applet Architecture

2.17. An Applet Skeleton

All but the most trivial applets override a set of methods that provides the basic mechanism by which the browser or applet viewer interfaces to the applet and controls its execution. Four of these methods, **init( )**, **start( )**, **stop( )**, and **destroy( )**, apply to all applets and are defined by **Applet**. Default implementations for all of these methods are provided. Applets do not need to override those methods they do not use. However, only very simple applets will not need to define all of them.

AWT-based applets (such as those discussed in this chapter) will also override the **paint( )** method, which is defined by the AWT **Component** class. This method is called when the applet's output must be redisplayed. (Swing-based applets use a different mechanism to accomplish this task.) These five methods can be assembled into the skeleton shown here:

```
// An Applet skeleton. import java.awt.*; import java.applet.*; /*
<applet code="AppletSkel" width=300 height=100> </applet>
*/
public class AppletSkel extends Applet { // Called first.
public void init() { // initialization
}
/*      Called second, after init(). Also called whenever the applet is restarted. */
public void start() {
// start or resume execution
}
// Called when the applet is stopped. public void stop() {
// suspends execution
}
/*      Called when applet is terminated. This is the last method executed. */
public void destroy() {
// perform shutdown activities
}
// Called when an applet's window must be restored. public void paint(Graphics g) {
// redisplay contents of window
}
}
```

Although this skeleton does not do anything, it can be compiled and run. When run, it generates the following window when viewed with an applet viewer:

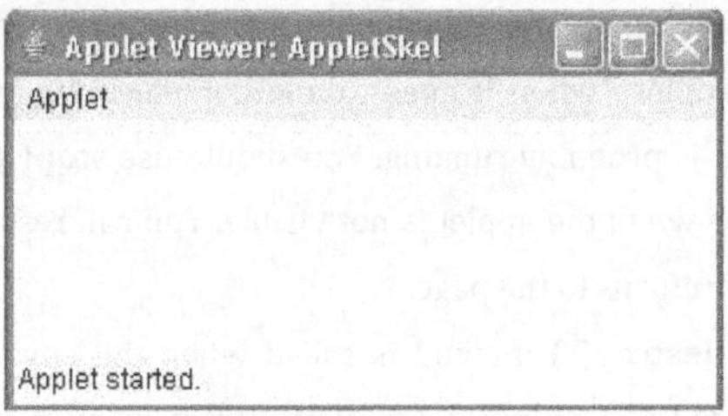

Applet Initialization and Termination

It is important to understand the order in which the various methods shown in the skeleton are called. When an applet begins, the following methods are called, in this sequence:

- init( )
- start( )
- paint( )

When an applet is terminated, the following sequence of method calls takes place:

- stop( )
- destroy( )

Let's look more closely at these methods.

- **init( )**:The **init( )** method is the first method to be called. This is where you should initialize variables. This method is called only once during the run time of your applet.
- **start( ):** The **start( )** method is called after **init( )**. It is also called to restart an applet after it has been stopped. Whereas **init( )** is called once-the first time an applet is loaded.
- **start( )** is called each time an applet's HTML document is displayed onscreen. So, if a user leaves a web page and comes back, the applet resumes execution at **start( )**.
- **paint( )**:The **paint( )** method is called each time your applet's output must be redrawn. This situation can occur for several reasons. For example, the window in which the applet is running may be overwritten by another window and then uncovered. Or the applet window may be minimized and then restored. **paint( )** is also called when the applet begins execution. Whatever the cause, whenever the applet must redraw its output, **paint( )** is called. The **paint( )** method has one parameter of type **Graphics**. This parameter will contain the graphics context, which describes the graphics environment in which the applet is running. This context is used whenever output to the applet is required.
- **stop( ):** The **stop( )** method is called when a web browser leaves the HTML document containing the applet—when it goes to another page, for example. When **stop( )** is called, the applet is probably running. You should use **stop( )** to suspend threads that don't need to run when the applet is not visible. You can restart them when **start( )** is called if the user returns to the page.
- **destroy( )**:The **destroy( )** method is called when the environment determines that your applet needs to be removed completely from memory. At this point, you should

free up any resources the applet may be using. The **stop( )** method is always called before **destroy( )**.

Overriding Update( )

In some situations, your applet may need to override another method defined by the AWT, called **update( )**. This method is called when your applet has requested that a portion of its window be redrawn. The default version of **update( )** simply calls **paint( )**. However, you can override the **update( )** method so that it performs more subtle repainting. In general, overriding **update( )** is a specialized technique that is not applicable to all applets, and the examples in this book do not override **update( )**.

2.18. Simple Applet Display Methods

As we all know that, applets are displayed in a window, and AWT-based applets use the AWT to perform input and output. Although we will examine the methods, procedures, and techniques necessary to fully handle the AWT windowed environment in subsequent chapters, a few are described here, because we will use them to write sample applets.

To output a string to an applet, use **drawString( )**, which is a member of the **Graphics** class. Typically, it is called from within either **update( )** or **paint( )**. It has the following general form:

```
void drawString(String message, int x, int y)
```

Here, *message* is the string to be output beginning at *x,y*. In a Java window, the upper-left corner is location 0,0. The **drawString( )** method will not recognize newline characters. If you want to start a line of text on another line, you must do so manually, specifying the precise X,Y location where you want the line to begin. (As you will see in later chapters, there are techniques that make this process easy.)

To set the background color of an applet's window, use **setBackground( )**. To set the foreground color (the color in which text is shown, for example), use **setForeground( )**. These methods are defined by **Component**, and they have the following general forms:

```
void setBackground(Color newColor)
void setForeground(Color newColor)
```

Here, newColor specifies the new color. The class Color defines the constants shown here that can be used to specify colors:

Color.black	Color.magenta
Color.blue	Color.orange
Color.cyan	Color.pink
Color.darkGray	Color.red

Uppercase versions of the constants are also defined.

The following example sets the background color to green and the text color to red:

```
setBackground(Color.green);
setForeground(Color.red);
```

A good place to set the foreground and background colors is in the **init( )** method. Of course, you can change these colors as often as necessary during the execution of the applet.

the current settings for the background and foreground colors can be obtained by calling **getBackground( )** and **getForeground( )**, respectively. They are also defined by **Component** and are shown here:

```
Color getBackground( )
Color getForeground( )
```

Here is a very simple applet that sets the background color to cyan, the foreground color to red, and displays a message that illustrates the order in which the **init( )**, **start( )**, and **paint( )** methods are called when an applet starts up:

```
/*    A simple applet that sets the foreground and background colors and outputs a string.
*/
import java.awt.*; import java.applet.*; /*
<applet code="Sample" width=300 height=50> </applet>
*/
public class Sample extends Applet{ String msg;
// set the foreground and background colors. public void init() {
setBackground(Color.cyan);
setForeground(Color.red); msg = "Inside init( ) --";
}
// Initialize the string to be displayed. public void start() {
msg += " Inside start( ) --";
}
// Display msg in applet window. public void paint(Graphics g) { msg += " Inside paint( ).";
g.drawString(msg, 10, 30);
}
}
```

This applet generates the window shown here:

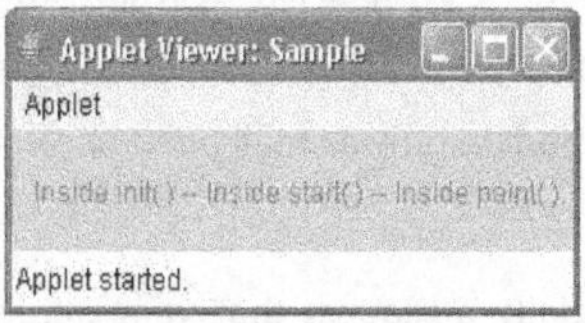

The methods **stop( )** and **destroy( )** are not overridden, because they are not needed by this simple applet.

2.19. Requesting Repainting

As a general rule, an applet writes to its window only when its **update( )** or **paint( )** method is called by the AWT. This raises an interesting question: How can the applet itself cause its window to be updated when its information changes? For example, if an applet is displaying a moving banner, what mechanism does the applet use to update the window each time this banner scrolls? Remember, one of the fundamental architectural constraints imposed on an applet is that it must quickly return control to the run-time system. It cannot create a loop inside **paint( )** that repeatedly scrolls the banner, for example. This would prevent control from passing back to the AWT. Given this constraint, it may seem that output to your applet's window will be difficult at best. Fortunately, this is not the case. Whenever your applet needs to update the information displayed in its window, it simply calls **repaint( )**.

The **repaint( )** method is defined by the AWT. It causes the AWT run-time system to execute a call to your applet's **update( )** method, which, in its default implementation, calls **paint( )**. Thus, for another part of your applet to output to its window, simply store the output and then call **repaint( )**. The AWT will then execute a call to **paint( )**, which can display the stored information. For example, if part of your applet needs to output a string, it can store this string in a **String** variable and then call **repaint( )**. Inside **paint( )**, you will output the string using **drawString( )**.

The **repaint( )** method has four forms. Let's look at each one, in turn. The simplest version of **repaint( )** is shown here:

void repaint( )

This version causes the entire window to be repainted. The following version specifies a region that will be repainted:

void repaint(int left, int top, int width, int height)

Here, the coordinates of the upper-left corner of the region are specified by *left* and *top,* and the width and height of the region are passed in *width* and *height.* These dimensions are specified in pixels. You save time by specifying a region to repaint. Window updates are costly in terms of time. If you need to update only a small portion of the window, it is more efficient to repaint only that region.

Calling **repaint( )** is essentially a request that your applet be repainted sometime soon. However, if your system is slow or busy, **update( )** might not be called immediately. Multiple requests for repainting that occur within a short time can be collapsed by the AWT in a manner such that **update( )** is only called sporadically. This can be a problem in many situations, including animation, in which a consistent update time is necessary. One solution to this problem is to use the following forms of **repaint( )**:

void repaint(long maxDelay)

void repaint(long maxDelay, int x, int y, int width, int height)

Here, *maxDelay* specifies the maximum number of milliseconds that can elapse before **update( )** is called. Beware, though. If the time elapses before **update( )** can be called, it isn't called. There's no return value or exception thrown, so you must be careful.

2.20. Using the Status Window

In addition to displaying information in its window, an applet can also output a message to the status window of the browser or applet viewer on which it is running. To do so, call **showStatus( )** with the string that you want displayed. The status window is a good place to give the user feedback about what is occurring in the applet, suggest options, or possibly report some types of errors. The status window also makes an excellent debugging aid, because it gives you an easy way to output information about your applet.

The following applet demonstrates **showStatus( )**:

```
// Using the Status Window. import java.awt.*;
import java.applet.*; /*
<applet code="StatusWindow" width=300 height=50> </applet>*/
public class StatusWindow extends Applet{ public void init() {
setBackground(Color.cyan);
}
// Display msg in applet window. public void paint(Graphics g) {
g.drawString("This is in the applet window.", 10, 20); showStatus("This is shown in the
```

```
status window.");
}
}
```

2.21. The HTML Applet Tag

Till now you have written some Applets and have run them in the browser or Appletviewer. You have used basic tags needed for running an Applet program. Now you will learn some more tag that contains various attributes.

2.22. Passing Parameters to Applets

As just discussed, the APPLET tag in HTML allows you to pass parameters to your applet. To retrieve a parameter, use the **getParameter( )** method. It returns the value of the specified parameter in the form of a **String** object. Thus, for numeric and **boolean** values, you will need to convert their string representations into their internal formats. Here is an example that demonstrates passing parameters:

```
// Use Parameters import java.awt.*; import java.applet.*; /*
<applet code="ParamDemo" width=300 height=80> <param name=fontName
value=Courier>
<param name=fontSize value=14> <param name=leading value=2>
<param name=accountEnabled value=true> </applet> */
public class ParamDemo extends Applet{ String fontName;
int fontSize; float leading; boolean active;
// Initialize the string to be displayed. public void start() {
String param;
fontName = getParameter("fontName"); if(fontName == null)
fontName = "Not Found";
param = getParameter("fontSize"); try {
if(param != null) // if not found fontSize = Integer.parseInt(param);
else
fontSize = 0;
} catch(NumberFormatException e) { fontSize = -1;
}
param = getParameter("leading"); try {
if(param != null) // if not found
leading = Float.valueOf(param).floatValue(); else
```

```
leading = 0;
} catch(NumberFormatException e) { leading = -1;
}
param = getParameter("accountEnabled"); if(param != null)
active = Boolean.valueOf(param).booleanValue();
}
// Display parameters.
public void paint(Graphics g) { g.drawString("Font name: " + fontName, 0, 10);
g.drawString("Font size: " + fontSize, 0, 26); g.drawString("Leading: " + leading, 0, 42);
g.drawString("Account Active: " + active, 0, 58);
}
}
```

Sample output from this program is shown here:

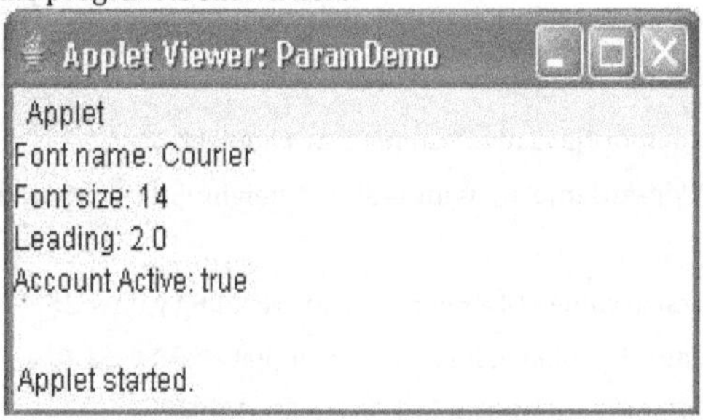

As the program shows, you should test the return values from **getParameter( )**. If a parameter isn't available, **getParameter( )** will return **null**. Also, conversions to numeric types must be attempted in a **try** statement that catches **NumberFormatException**. Uncaught exceptions should never occur within an applet.

2.23. GETDOCUMENTBASE() and GETCODEBASE()

Often, you will create applets that will need to explicitly load media and text. Java will allow the applet to load data from the directory holding the HTML file that started the applet (the *document base*) and the directory from which the applet's class file was loaded (the *code base*).

These directories are returned as **URL** objects (described in Chapter 20) by **getDocumentBase( )** and **getCodeBase( )**. They can be concatenated with a string that names the file you want to load. To actually load another file, you will use the **showDocument( )** method defined by the **AppletContext** interface, discussed in the next section.

The following applet illustrates these methods:

```
// Display code and document bases. import java.awt.*;
import java.applet.*; import java.net.*;
/*
<applet code="Bases" width=300 height=50> </applet>
*/
public class Bases extends Applet{ // Display code and document bases. public void
paint(Graphics g) {
String msg;
URL url = getCodeBase(); // get code base msg = "Code base: " + url.toString();
g.drawString(msg, 10, 20);
url = getDocumentBase(); // get document base msg = "Document base: " + url.toString();
g.drawString(msg, 10, 40);
}
}
```

Sample output from this program is shown here

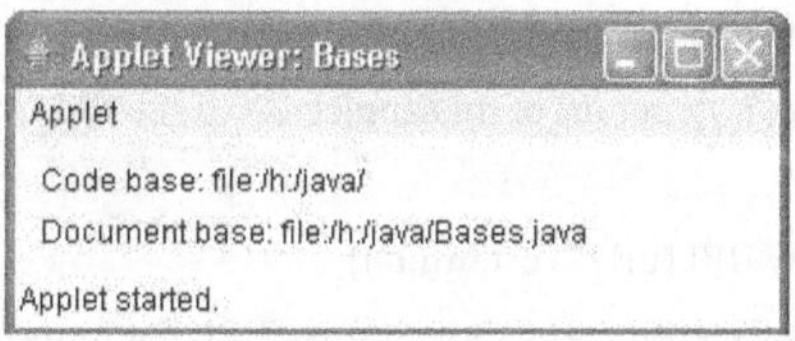

2.24. Apletcontext and Showdocument()

One application of Java is to use active images and animation to provide a graphical means of navigating the Web that is more interesting than simple text-based links. To allow your applet to transfer control to another URL, you must use the **showDocument( )** method defined by the **AppletContext** interface. **AppletContext** is an interface that lets you get information from the applet's execution environment. The methods defined by **AppletContext** are shown in Table 21-2. The context of the currently executing applet is obtained by a call to the **getAppletContext( )** method defined by **Applet**. Within an applet, once you have obtained the applet's context, you can bring another document into view by calling **showDocument( )**. This method has no return value and throws no exception if it fails, so use it carefully. There are two **showDocument( )** methods. The method **showDocument(URL)** displays the document at the specified **URL**. The method **showDocument(URL, String)** displays the specified document at the specified location within the browser window. Valid arguments for *where* are "_self" (show in current frame), "_parent" (show in parent frame), "_top" (show in topmost frame), and "_blank" (show in new browser window). You can also specify a name, which causes the document to be shown in a new browser window by that name.

The following applet demonstrates **AppletContext** and **showDocument( )**. Upon execution, it obtains the current applet context and uses that context to transfer control to a file called **Test.html**. This file must be in the same directory as the applet. **Test.html** can contain any valid hypertext that you like.

```
/* Using an applet context, getCodeBase(),
and showDocument() to display an HTML file.
*/
import java.awt.*; import java.applet.*; import java.net.*;
/*
<applet code="ACDemo" width=300 height=50> </applet>
*/
public class ACDemo extends Applet{ public void start() {
AppletContext ac = getAppletContext();
URL url = getCodeBase(); // get url of this applet
try {
ac.showDocument(new URL(url+"Test.html"));
} catch(MalformedURLException e) { showStatus("URL not found");
}
}
}
```

Method	Description
Applet getApplet(String *appletName*)	Returns the applet specified by *appletName* if it is within the current applet context. Otherwise, null is returned.
Enumeration<Applet> getApplets( )	Returns an enumeration that contains all of the applets within the current applet context.
AudioClip getAudioClip(URL *url*)	Returns an AudioClip object that encapsulates the audio clip found at the location specified by *url*.
Image getImage(URL *url*)	Returns an Image object that encapsulates the image found at the location specified by *url*.
InputStream getStream(String *key*)	Returns the stream linked to *key*. Keys are linked to streams by using the setStream( ) method. A null reference is returned if no stream is linked to *key*.
Iterator<String> getStreamKeys( )	Returns an iterator for the keys associated with the invoking object. The keys are linked to streams. See getStream( ) and setStream( ).
void setStream(String *key*, InputStream *strm*)	Links the stream specified by *strm* to the key passed in *key*. The *key* is deleted from the invoking object if *strm* is null.
void showDocument(URL *url*)	Brings the document at the URL specified by *url* into view. This method may not be supported by applet viewers.
void showDocument(URL *url*, String *where*)	Brings the document at the URL specified by *url* into view. This method may not be supported by applet viewers. The placement of the document is specified by *where* as described in the text.
void showStatus(String *str*)	Displays *str* in the status window.

2.25. The Audioclip Interface

The **AudioClip** interface defines these methods: **play( )** (play a clip from the beginning), **stop( )** (stop playing the clip), and **loop( )** (play the loop continuously). After you have loaded an audio clip using **getAudioClip( )**, you can use these methods to play it.

2.26. The Appletstub Interface

The **AppletStub** interface provides the means by which an applet and the browser (or applet viewer) communicate. Your code will not typically implement this interface.

2.27. Outputting to the Console

Although output to an applet's window must be accomplished through GUI-based methods, such as **drawString( )**, it is still possible to use console output in your applet—especially for debugging purposes. In an applet, when you call a method such as **System.out.println( )**, the output is not sent to your applet's window. Instead, it appears either in the console session in which you launched the applet viewer or in the Java console that is available in some browsers. Use of console output for purposes other than debugging is discouraged, since it violates the design principles of the graphical interface most users will expect.

2.28. Summary

This unit is designed to know about the graphical interfaces in Java. In this unit you become familiar with classes, constructors, AWT, which are used to add components in the container or a kind of tray.

2.29. Questions

1. Differentiate C++ language and Java language with respect to inheritance and also mention the use of super and this in JAVA inheritance?
2. Discuss the following

   i. Inner Classes ii. Overriding and Overloading
3. Briefly explain the role of interface while implementing multiple inheritance in JAVA?
4. What is alternative approach to implement multiple inheritance in Java? Explain, with an example?
5. What are applets? Explain different stages in the cycle of an applet?
6. Explain the applet architecture and demonstrate how to pass parameter for font size, font name and type conversion in applets
7. What is an inner class? Write a program to demonstrate inner class?

8. Explain the java's built in exceptions?
9. Define exception. Demonstrate the working of nested try blocks, with suitable examples.
10. Write short notes on

    i. Final class ii. Abstract class
11. With example give two uses of super.
12. Write a program which contains one method which will throw IllegalAccesException and use proper exception handlers so that exception should be printed?
13. What are the two types of applet? Explain the skeleton of an applet. Enlist the applet tags?
14. What the different forms of repaint method.
15. What is meant by instance variable hiding? How to overcome it?
16. Write a program to implement a stack that can hold 10 integer values?
17. What is an exception give an example for nested try statements?
18. List Applet initialization and termination methods. Write a Java Applet that sets the background color to cyan and foreground color to red and outputs a string message "A Simple Applet"?
19. Explain the constructor method. How it differs from other member function.
20. Explain the exception handling mechanism with an example?

UNIT–3

MULTI THREADED PROGRAMMING, EVENT HANDLING

3.1. Introduction

Those who are familiar with the modern operating systems such as Windows 95 and windows XP may recognize that they can executive many programs simultaneously. This ability is known as multitasking. In system terminology it is called multithreading. Multithreading is a conceptual programming paradigm where a program (process) is divided into two or more subprograms (processes), which can be implemented at the same time in parallel. For example, one subprogram can display an animation on the screen while another may build the next animation to be displayed.

A unique property of java is its support for multithreading. That is, java enables us to use multiple flows of control in developing programs. Each flow of control may be thought of as a separate program known as a thread that runs in parallel to others. A program that contains multiple flows of control is known as multithreaded program.

3.2. Objective

After Going through This Unit, you should be able to

- Describe the concept of multithreading.
- Explain the Java thread model.
- Create and use threads in program.
- Describe how to set the thread priorities.
- Use the concept of synchronization in programming, and
- Use inter-thread communication in programs.
- Explain the concept of Bounded Buffer Problem, Read Write Problem and Producer Consumer Problem.
- Explain the concept of Event handling
- Use various Listeners class and Adapter classes.

3.3. Multi Threaded Programming

Java is a multithreaded programming language which means we can develop multithreaded program using Java. A multithreaded program contains two or more parts that can run concurrently and each part can handle different task at the same time making optimal use of the available resources especially when your computer has multiple CPUs.

By definition multitasking is when multiple processes share common processing resources such as a CPU. Multithreading extends the idea of multitasking into applications where you can subdivide specific operations within a single application into individual threads. Each of the threads can run in parallel. The OS divides processing time not only among different applications, but also among each thread within an application.

Multithreading enables you to write in a way where multiple activities can proceed concurrently in the same program.

Life Cycle of a Thread: A thread goes through various stages in its life cycle. For example, a thread is born, started, runs, and then dies. Following diagram shows complete life cycle of a thread.

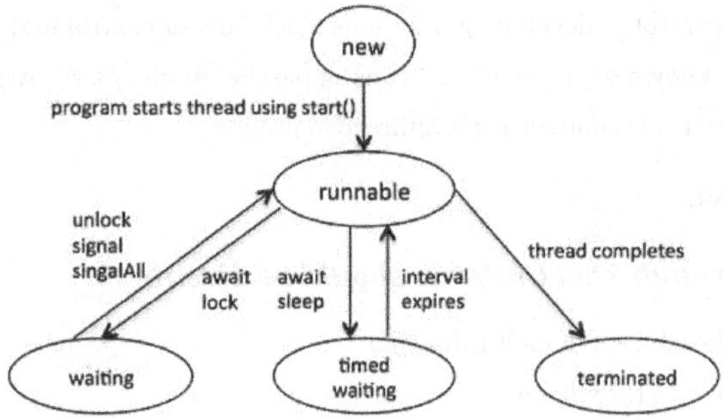

- **New:** A new thread begins its life cycle in the new state. It remains in this state until the program starts the thread. It is also referred to as a born thread.
- **Runnable:** After a newly born thread is started, the thread becomes runnable. A thread in this state is considered to be executing its task.
- **Waiting:** Sometimes, a thread transitions to the waiting state while the thread waits for another thread to perform a task. A thread transitions back to the runnable state only when another thread signals the waiting thread to continue executing.
- **Timed waiting:** A runnable thread can enter the timed waiting state for a specified interval of time. A thread in this state transitions back to the runnable state when that time interval expires or when the event it is waiting for occurs.
- **Terminated:** A runnable thread enters the terminated state when it completes its task or otherwise terminates.

Thread Priorities

Every Java thread has a priority that helps the operating system determine the order in which threads are scheduled.

Java thread priorities are in the range between MIN_PRIORITY (a constant of 1) and MAX_PRIORITY (a constant of 10). By default, every thread is given priority NORM_PRIORITY (a constant of 5).

Threads with higher priority are more important to a program and should be allocated processor time before lower-priority threads. However, thread priorities cannot guarantee the order in which threads execute and very much platform dependent.

3.4. What Are Threads

Multithreading refers to two or more tasks executing concurrently within a single program. A **thread** is an independent path of execution within a program. Many threads can run concurrently within a program. Every thread in Java is created and controlled by the **java.lang.Thread class**. A Java program can have many threads, and these threads can run concurrently, either asynchronously or synchronously.

Multithreading has several advantages over Multiprocessing such as;

- Threads are lightweight compared to processes
- Threads share the same address space and therefore can share both data and code
- Context switching between threads is usually less expensive than between processes
- Cost of thread intercommunication is relatively low that that of process intercommunication
- Threads allow different tasks to be performed concurrently.

3.5. How to Make the Classes Threadable

There are two ways to create thread in java or make the class threadable.

- Implement the Runnable interface (java.lang.Runnable)
- By Extending the Thread class (java.lang.Thread)

3.5.1. Extending Threads

The procedure for creating threads based on extending the Thread is as follows:

- A class extending the Thread class overrides the run() method from the Thread class to define the code executed by the thread.

- This subclass may call a Thread constructor explicitly in its constructors to initialize the thread, using the super() call.
- The start() method inherited from the Thread class is invoked on the object of the class to make the thread eligible for running.

Below is a program that illustrates instantiation and running of threads by extending the Thread class instead of implementing the Runnable interface. To start the thread you need to invoke the start() method on your object.

```
class XThread extends Thread {
        XThread() {
        }
        XThread(String threadName) {
                super(threadName); // Initialize thread.
                System.out.println(this);
                start();
        }
        public void run() {
                //Display info about this particular thread
                System.out.println(Thread.currentThread().getName());

        }
}
public class ThreadExample {
        public static void main(String[] args) {
                Thread thread1 = new Thread(new XThread(), "thread1");
                Thread thread2 = new Thread(new XThread(), "thread2");
                // The below 2 threads are assigned default names
                Thread thread3 = new XThread();
                Thread thread4 = new XThread();
                Thread thread5 = new XThread("thread5");
                //Start the threads
                thread1.start();
                thread2.start();
                thread3.start();
                thread4.start();
                try {
```

```
//The sleep() method is invoked on the main thread to cause a one second delay.
    Thread.currentThread().sleep(1000);
    } catch (InterruptedException e) {
    }
    //Display info about the main thread
    System.out.println(Thread.currentThread());
    }
    }
```

Output:

```
    Thread[thread5,5,main]
    thread1
    thread5
    thread2
    Thread-3
    Thread-2
    Thread[main,5,main]
```

3.5.2. Implementing Runnable

The Runnable Interface Signature

```
    public interface Runnable {
    void run();
    }
```

One way to create a thread in java is to implement the Runnable Interface and then instantiate an object of the class. We need to override the run() method into our class which is the only method that needs to be implemented. The run() method contains the logic of the thread.

The Procedure for Creating Threads Based on the Runnable Interface is as follows

- A class implements the Runnable interface, providing the run() method that will be executed by the thread. An object of this class is a Runnable object.
- An object of Thread class is created by passing a Runnable object as argument to the Thread constructor. The Thread object now has a Runnable object that implements the run() method.
- The start() method is invoked on the Thread object created in the previous step. The start() method returns immediately after a thread has been spawned.

- The thread ends when the run() method ends, either by normal completion or by throwing an uncaught exception.

Below is a program that illustrates instantiation and running of threads using the runnable interface instead of extending the Thread class. To start the thread you need to invoke the **start()** method on your object.

```
class RunnableThread implements Runnable {
        Thread runner;
        public RunnableThread() {
        }
        public RunnableThread(String threadName) {
        runner = new Thread(this, threadName); // (1) Create a new thread.
        System.out.println(runner.getName());
        runner.start(); // (2) Start the thread.
        }
        public void run() {
                //Display info about this particular thread
                System.out.println(Thread.currentThread());
        }
}
public class RunnableExample {
public static void main(String[] args) {
        Thread thread1 = new Thread(new RunnableThread(), "thread1");
        Thread thread2 = new Thread(new RunnableThread(), "thread2");
        RunnableThread thread3 = new RunnableThread("thread3");
                //Start the threads
                thread1.start();
                thread2.start();
                try {
                        //delay for one second
                        Thread.currentThread().sleep(1000);
                } catch (InterruptedException e) {
                }
                //Display info about the main thread
                System.out.println(Thread.currentThread());
        }
}
```

Thread Methods

Following is the list of important methods available in the Thread class.

S.No	Methods with Description
1	**public void start()** Starts the thread in a separate path of execution, then invokes the run() method on this Thread object.
2	**public void run()** If this Thread object was instantiated using a separate Runnable target, the run() method is invoked on that Runnable object.
3	**public final void setName(String name)** Changes the name of the Thread object. There is also a getName() method for retrieving the name.
4	**public final void setPriority(int priority)** Sets the priority of this Thread object. The possible values are between 1 and 10.
5	**public final void setDaemon(boolean on)** A parameter of true denotes this Thread as a daemon thread.
6	**public final void join(long millisec)** The current thread invokes this method on a second thread, causing the current thread to block until the second thread terminates or the specified number of milliseconds passes.
7	**public void interrupt()** Interrupts this thread, causing it to continue execution if it was blocked for any reason.
8	**public final boolean is Alive()** Returns true if the thread is alive, which is any time after the thread has been started but before it runs to completion.

The previous methods are invoked on a particular Thread object. The following methods in the Thread class are static. Invoking one of the static methods performs the operation on the currently running thread.

S.No	Methods with Description
1	**public static void yield()** Causes the currently running thread to yield to any other threads of the same priority that are waiting to be scheduled.
2	**public static void sleep(long millisec)** Causes the currently running thread to block for at least the specified number of milliseconds.
3	**public static boolean holdsLock(Object x)** Returns true if the current thread holds the lock on the given Object.
4	**public static Thread currentThread()** Returns a reference to the currently running thread, which is the thread that invokes this method.
5	**public static void dumpStack()** Prints the stack trace for the currently running thread, which is useful when debugging a multithreaded application.

3.6. Synchronization

When we start two or more threads within a program, there may be a situation when multiple threads try to access the same resource and finally they can produce unforeseen result due to concurrency issue. For example if multiple threads try to write within a same file then they may corrupt the data because one of the threads can overwrite data or while one thread is opening the same file at the same time another thread might be closing the same file.

So there is a need to synchronize the action of multiple threads and make sure that only one thread can access the resource at a given point in time. This is implemented using a concept called **monitors.** Each object in Java is associated with a monitor, which a thread can lock or unlock. Only one thread at a time may hold a lock on a monitor.

Java programming language provides a very handy way of creating threads and synchronizing their task by using **synchronized** blocks. You keep shared resources within this block. Following is the general form of the synchronized statement:

```
synchronized(objectidentifier)
{
 // Access shared variables and other shared resources
}
```

Here, the **objectidentifier** is a reference to an object whose lock associates with the monitor that the synchronized statement represents.

3.6.1 Multithreading Example without Synchronization

Here is a simple example which may or may not print counter value in sequence and every time we run it, it produces different result based on CPU availability to a thread.

```
class PrintDemo {
  public void printCount(){
   try {
      for(int i = 5; i > 0; i--) {
         System.out.println("Counter  ---  " + i );
      }
   } catch (Exception e) {
      System.out.println("Thread interrupted.");
   }
  }
}
class ThreadDemo extends Thread {
  private Thread t;
  private String threadName;
  PrintDemo  PD;
```

```
  ThreadDemo( String name,  PrintDemo pd){
     threadName = name;
     PD = pd;
  }
  public void run() {
    PD.printCount();
    System.out.println("Thread " +  threadName + " exiting.");
  }
  public void start ()
  {
    System.out.println("Starting " +  threadName );
    if (t == null)
    {
      t = new Thread (this, threadName);
      t.start ();
    }
  }
}
public class TestThread {
  public static void main(String args[]) {
    PrintDemo PD = new PrintDemo();
    ThreadDemo T1 = new ThreadDemo("Thread - 1 ", PD );
    ThreadDemo T2 = new ThreadDemo("Thread - 2 ", PD );
    T1.start();
    T2.start();
    // wait for threads to end
    try {
      T1.join();
      T2.join();
    } catch( Exception e) {
      System.out.println("Interrupted");
    }
  }
}
```

3.6.2 *Multithreading Example with Synchronization*

Here is the same example which prints counter value in sequence and every time we run it, it produces same result.

```
class PrintDemo {
  public void printCount(){
   try {
      for(int i = 5; i > 0; i--) {
        System.out.println("Counter   ---   " + i );
      }
   } catch (Exception e) {
      System.out.println("Thread  interrupted.");
   }
  }
}
class ThreadDemo extends Thread {
  private Thread t;
  private String threadName;
  PrintDemo  PD;
  ThreadDemo( String name,  PrintDemo pd){
    threadName = name;
    PD = pd;
  }
  public void run() {
   synchronized(PD) {
     PD.printCount();
   }
   System.out.println("Thread " +  threadName + " exiting.");
  }
  public void start ()
  {
   System.out.println("Starting " +  threadName );
   if (t == null)
```

```
    {
      t = new Thread (this, threadName);
      t.start ();
    }
  }
}
public class TestThread {
  public static void main(String args[]) {
    PrintDemo PD = new PrintDemo();
    ThreadDemo T1 = new ThreadDemo( "Thread - 1 ", PD );
    ThreadDemo T2 = new ThreadDemo( "Thread - 2 ", PD );
    T1.start();
    T2.start();
    // wait for threads to end
    try {
      T1.join();
      T2.join();
    } catch( Exception e) {
      System.out.println("Interrupted");
    }
  }
}
```

3.7. Changing State of the Thread

A thread can be in one of the following states:

- **New:** A thread that has not yet started is in this state.
- **Runnable:** A thread executing in the Java virtual machine is in this state.
- **Blocked:** A thread that is blocked waiting for a monitor lock is in this state.
- **Waiting:** A thread that is waiting indefinitely for another thread to perform a particular action is in this state.
- **timed_waiting:** A thread that is waiting for another thread to perform an action for up to a specified waiting time is in this state.
- **Terminated:** A thread that has exited is in this state.

3.8. Bounded Buffer Problems

Refer Class Notes

3.9. Read-Write Problem

Refer Class Notes

3.10. Producer- Consumer Problems

Problem

- This problem is also known as **bounded buffer problem**, well known problem of multi-process synchronization.
- The problem describes two processes who shares a common, fixed-size buffer or array as a queue. :
  - **Producer** : Generates a piece of data and put it into the buffer (one element at a time).
  - **Consumer** : Consumes the data or removes data from the buffer (one element at a time).
- The Problem is to make sure that
  - Producer shouldn't try to add data into the buffer if it's full.
  - Consumer shouldn't try to remove data from an empty buffer.

Solution

Producer Should

- Go to sleep or discard data if the buffer is full.
- Next time when the consumer removes an item from the buffer, It will notifies the **producer**, And starts to fill the buffer again.

Consumer Should

- Go to sleep if it finds the buffer to be empty.
- Next time when the producer puts data into the buffer, It will wakes up the sleeping **consumer**, And starts consuming the buffer again.
- The solution can be reached by means of **inter-process communication**, typically using semaphores/monitor/lock.
- An **inadequate solution could result in a deadlock** where both processes are waiting to be awakened.

Example

```
public class ProducerConsumerProblem {
  public static void main(String[] args) {
    // buffer
    final Buffer buffer = new Buffer();
    // producer thread
    Thread producer = new Thread(new Runnable() {
      public void run() {
        for (int i = 0; i < 10; i++) {
          try {
            buffer.put(i);
          } catch (InterruptedException e) {
            e.printStackTrace();
          }
        }
      }
    });
    // consumer thread
    Thread consumer = new Thread(new Runnable() {
      public void run() {
        for (int i = 0; i < 10; i++) {
          try {
            buffer.get();
          } catch (InterruptedException e) {
            e.printStackTrace();
          }
        }
      }
    });
    producer.start();
    consumer.start();
  }
}
class Buffer {
  private static final int BUFFER_SIZE = 5;
  private int[] bufferArray = new int[BUFFER_SIZE];
```

```
    private int counter = -1;
    private boolean BUFFER_FULL = false;
    private boolean BUFFER_EMPTY = true;
    public synchronized void put(int value) throws InterruptedException {
        if (counter >= (BUFFER_SIZE-1)) {
            System.out.println("Buffer is full.. Wait, Thread ID: "
                    + Thread.currentThread().getId());
            BUFFER_FULL = true;
            wait();
        }
        counter++;
        bufferArray[counter] = value;
        System.out.println("put : bufferArray[" + counter + "] = " + value);
        if (BUFFER_EMPTY) {
            BUFFER_EMPTY = false;
            notify();
        }
    }
    public synchronized int get() throws InterruptedException {
        if (counter < 0) {
            System.out.println("Buffer is empty.. Wait, Thread ID: "
                    + Thread.currentThread().getId());
            BUFFER_EMPTY = true;
            wait();
        }
        int value = bufferArray[counter];
        System.out.println("get : bufferArray[" + counter + "] = " + value);
        counter--;
        if (BUFFER_FULL) {
            BUFFER_FULL = false;
            notify();
        }
        return value;
    }
}
```

3.11. Event Handling

Event handling is fundamental to Java programming because it is integral to the creation of applets and other types of GUI-based programs. We know that applets are event-driven programs that use a graphical user interface to interact with the user. Furthermore, any program that uses a graphical user interface, such as a Java application written for Windows, is event driven. Events are supported by a number of packages, including **java.util**, **java.awt**, and **java.awt.event.**

Most events to our program will respond are generated when the user interacts with a GUI-based program. Events are passed to the program in a variety of ways, with the specific method dependent upon the actual event. There are several types of events, including those generated by the mouse, the keyboard, and various GUI controls, such as a push button, scroll bar, or check box.

3.12. Two Event Handling Mechanisms

Before beginning our discussion of event handling, an important point must be made: The way in which events are handled changed significantly between the original version of Java (1.0) and modern versions of Java, beginning with version 1.1. The 1.0 method of event handling is still supported, but it is not recommended for new programs. Also, many of the methods that support the old 1.0 event model have been deprecated.

3.13. The Delegation Event Model

The modern approach to handling events is based on the *delegation event model,* which defines standard and consistent mechanisms to generate and process events. A source generates an event and sends it to one or more listeners. Then, the listener simply waits until it receives an event. Once an event is received, the listener processes the event and then returns.

The advantage of this design is that the application logic that processes events is cleanly separated from the user interface logic that generates those events. A user interface element is able to "delegate" the processing of an event to a separate piece of code.

In the delegation event model, listeners must register with a source in order to receive an event notification. Notifications are sent only to listeners that want to receive them.

3.14. Event Classes

The classes that represent events are at the core of Java's event handling mechanism. The most widely used events are those defined by the AWT and those defined by Swing.

EventObject class is the super class of all the events, it is in **java.util**. EventObject class has one constructor which is shown below:

EventObject(Object *src*)

Here, src is the object that generates this event.

EventObject contains two methods: **getSource( )** and **toString( )**.

- **getSource( )** method returns the source of the event. Its general form is shown here:

  Object getSource( )

- **toString( )** returns the string equivalent of the event.

AWTEvent class is defined within the **java.awt** package; it is a subclass of **EventObject.**

AWTEvent is the super class (either directly or indirectly) of all AWT-based events used by the delegation event model. **getID( )** method can be used to determine the type of the event. The signature of this method is shown here:

int getID( )

3.15. Sources of Events

A source is an object that generates an event. Sources may generate more than one type of event. A source must register listeners in order for the listeners to receive notifications about a specific type of event. Each type of event has its own registration method. Here is the general form:

public void addTypeListener(TypeListener el)

Here, Type is the name of the event, and *el* is a reference to the event listener.

For example: The method that registers a keyboard event listener is called *addKeyListener( ).* The method that registers a mouse motion listener is called **addMouseMotionListener( ).** When an event occurs, all registered listeners are notified and receive a copy of the event object. Some sources may allow only one listener to register. The general form of such a method is this:

public void **addTypeListener(TypeListener el)** throws java.util. Too Many Listeners Exception Here, Type is the name of the event, and el is a reference to the event listener. When such an event occurs, the registered listener is notified. This is known as uni casting the event.

A source also provide a method for listener to unregister an interest in a specific type of event. The general form of such a method is this:

public void removeTypeListener(TypeListener el)

Here, Type is the name of the event, and el is a reference to the event listener.

For example: To remove a keyboard listener, call **removeKeyListener( ).**

The methods that add or remove listeners are provided by the source that generates events.

Table below Lists Some of the User Interface Components that can Generate the Event

Event Source	Description
Button	Generates action events when the button is pressed.
Check box	Generates item events when the check box is selected or deselected.
Choice	Generates item events when the choice is changed.
List	Generates action events when an item is double-clicked; generates item events when an item is selected or deselected.
Menu Item	Generates action events when a menu item is selected; generates item events when a checkable menu item is selected or deselected.
Scroll bar	Generates adjustment events when the scroll bar is manipulated.
Text components	Generates text events when the user enters a character.
Window	Generates window events when a window is activated, closed, deactivated, deiconified, iconified, opened, or quit.

3.16. Event Listener Interfaces

A listener is an object that is notified when an event occurs. It has two major requirements.

- It must have been registered with one or more sources to receive notifications about specific types of events.
- It must implement methods to receive and process these notifications.

The methods that receive and process events are defined in a set of interfaces found in **java.awt.event.**

For Example

The **MouseMotionListener** interface defines two methods to receive notifications when the mouse is dragged or moved.

Listeners are created by implementing one or more of the interfaces defined by the **java.awt.event** package.

The following table shows the interfaces

Interface	Description
ActionListener	Defines one method to receive action events.
AdjustmentListener	Defines one method to receive adjustment events.
ComponentListener	Defines four methods to recognize when a component is hidden, moved, resized, or shown.
ContainerListener	Defines two methods to recognize when a component is added to or removed from a container.
FocusListener	Defines two methods to recognize when a component gains or loses keyboard focus.
ItemListener	Defines one method to recognize when the state of an item changes.
KeyListener	Defines three methods to recognize when a key is pressed, released, or typed.
MouseListener	Defines five methods to recognize when the mouse is clicked, enters a component, exits a component, is pressed, or is released.
MouseMotionListener	Defines two methods to recognize when the mouse is dragged or moved.
MouseWheelListener	Defines one method to recognize when the mouse wheel is moved.
TextListener	Defines one method to recognize when a text value changes.
WindowFocusListener	Defines two methods to recognize when a window gains or loses input focus.
WindowListener	Defines seven methods to recognize when a window is activated, closed, deactivated, deiconified, iconified, opened, or quit.

The following sections examine the specific methods that are contained in each interface.

- **The ActionListener Interface:** This interface defines the **actionPerformed( )** method that is invoked when an action event occurs. Its general form is shown here:
  void actionPerformed(ActionEvent *ae*)
- **The AdjustmentListener Interface:** This interface defines the **adjustmentValueChanged( )** method that is invoked when an adjustment event occurs. Its general form is shown here:
  void adjustmentValueChanged(AdjustmentEvent *ae*)
- **The ComponentListener Interface:** This interface defines four methods that are invoked when a component is resized, moved, shown, or hidden. Their general forms are shown here:
  void componentResized(ComponentEvent *ce*)
  void componentMoved(ComponentEvent *ce*)
  void componentShown(ComponentEvent *ce*)
  void componentHidden(ComponentEvent *ce*)
- **The ContainerListener Interface:** This interface contains two methods. When a component is added to a container, **componentAdded( )** is invoked. When a component is removed from a container, **componentRemoved( )** is invoked. Their general forms are shown here:
  void componentAdded(ContainerEvent ce)
  void componentRemoved(ContainerEvent ce)

- **The FocusListener** Interface: This interface defines two methods. When a component obtains keyboard focus, **focusGained( )** is invoked. When a component loses keyboard focus, **focusLost( )** is called. Their general forms are shown here:
  void focusGained(FocusEvent fe)
  void focusLost(FocusEvent fe)
- **The ItemListener Interface:** This interface defines the **itemStateChanged( )** method that is invoked when the state of an item changes. Its general form is shown here:
  void itemStateChanged(ItemEvent ie)
- **The KeyListener Interface:** This interface defines three methods. The **keyPressed( )** and **keyReleased( )** methods are invoked when a key is pressed and released, respectively. The **keyTyped( )** method is invoked when a character has been entered.
  For example, if a user presses and releases the A key, three events are generated in sequence: **key pressed, typed, and released.** If a user presses and releases the HOME key, two key events are generated in sequence: **key pressed and released.**
  The general forms of these methods are shown here:
  void keyPressed(KeyEvent *ke*)
  void keyReleased(KeyEvent *ke*)
  void keyTyped(KeyEvent *ke*)
- **The MouseListener Interface:** This interface defines five methods. If the mouse is pressed and released at the same point, mouseClicked( ) is invoked. When the mouse enters a component, the mouseEntered( ) method is called. When it leaves, mouseExited( ) is called. The mousePressed( ) and mouseReleased( ) methods are invoked when the mouse is pressed and released, respectively.
  The general forms of these methods are shown here:
  void mouseClicked(MouseEvent *me*)
  void mouseEntered(MouseEvent *me*)
  void mouseExited(MouseEvent *me*)
  void mousePressed(MouseEvent *me*)
  void mouseReleased(MouseEvent *me*)
- **The MouseMotionListener Interface**:This interface defines two methods. The mouseDragged( ) method is called multiple times as the mouse is dragged. The **mouseMoved( )** method is called multiple times as the mouse is moved.
  Their general forms are shown here:
  void mouseDragged(MouseEvent *me*)

void mouseMoved(MouseEvent *me*)

- **The MouseWheelListener Interface:** This interface defines the **mouseWheelMoved( )** method that is invoked when the mouse wheel is moved.

  Its general form is shown here:

  void mouseWheelMoved(MouseWheelEvent mwe)

- **The TextListener Interface**:This interface defines the textChanged( ) method that is invoked when a change occurs in a text area or text field.

  Its general form is shown here:

  void textChanged(TextEvent *te*)

- **The WindowFocusListener Interface:**This interface defines two methods: windowGainedFocus( ) and windowLostFocus( ). These are called when a window gains or loses input focus.

  Their general forms are shown here:

  void windowGainedFocus(WindowEvent *we*)

  void windowLostFocus(WindowEvent *we*)

- **The WindowListener Interface:**This interface defines seven methods. The windowActivated( ) and windowDeactivated( ) methods are invoked when a window is activated or deactivated, respectively. If a window is iconified, the windowIconified( ) method is called. When a window is deiconified, the windowDeiconified( ) method is called. When a window is opened or closed, the windowOpened( ) or windowClosed( ) methods are called, respectively. The windowClosing( ) method is called when a window is being closed.

  The general forms of these methods are:

  void windowActivated(WindowEvent *we*)

  void windowClosed(WindowEvent *we*)

  void windowClosing(WindowEvent *we*)

  void windowDeactivated(WindowEvent we)

  void windowDeiconified(WindowEvent we)

  void windowIconified(WindowEvent *we*)

  void windowOpened(WindowEvent *we*)

3.17. Using the Delegation Event Model

The modern approach to handling events is based on the delegation event model, which defines standard and consistent mechanisms to generate and process events. Its concept is quite simple: a source generates an event and sends it to one or more listeners. In this scheme, the listener simply waits until it receives an event. Once an event is received, the listener processes the event and then returns. The advantage of this design is that the application logic that processes events is cleanly separated from the user interface logic that generates those events. A user interface element is able to "delegate" the processing of an event to a separate piece of code.

In the delegation event model, listeners must register with a source in order to receive an event notification. This provides an important benefit: notifications are sent only to listeners that want to receive them. This is a more efficient way to handle events than the design used by the old Java 1.0 approach. Previously, an event was propagated up the containment hierarchy until it was handled by a component. This required components to receive events that they did not process, and it wasted valuable time. The delegation event model eliminates this overhead.

3.18. Adapter Classes

Java provides a special feature, called an *adapter class,* that can simplify the creation of event handlers in certain situations. An adapter class provides an empty implementation of all methods in an event listener interface. Adapter classes are useful when we want to receive and process only some of the events that are handled by a particular event listener interface. We can define a new class to act as an event listener by extending one of the adapter classes and implementing only those events in which you are interested.

For example, the **MouseMotionAdapter** class has two methods, **mouseDragged( )** and **mouseMoved( )**, which are the methods defined by the **MouseMotionListener** interface. If you were interested in only mouse drag events, then you could simply extend **MouseMotionAdapter** and override **mouseDragged( )**. The empty implementation of **mouseMoved( )** would handle the mouse motion events for you.

Table below lists the commonly used adapter classes in **java.awt.event** and notes the interface that each implements.

The following example demonstrates an adapter. It displays a message in the status bar of an applet viewer or browser when the mouse is clicked or dragged. However, all other mouse events are silently ignored. The program has three classes. **AdapterDemo** extends **Applet**. Its **init( )** method creates an instance of **MyMouseAdapter** and registers that object to receive notifications of mouse events. It also creates an instance of **MyMouseMotionAdapter** and registers that object to receive notifications of mouse motion events. Both of the constructors take a reference to the applet as an argument.

MyMouseAdapter extends **MouseAdapter** and overrides the **mouseClicked( )** method. The other mouse events are silently ignored by code inherited from the **MouseAdapter** class. **MyMouseMotionAdapter** extends **MouseMotionAdapter** and overrides the **mouseDragged( )** method. The other mouse motion event is silently ignored by code inherited from the **MouseMotionAdapter** class.

```
// Demonstrate an adapter. Import java.awt.*;
import java.awt.event.*; import java.applet.*;
/*<applet code="AdapterDemo" width=300 height=100> </applet> */
public class AdapterDemo extends Applet { public void init() {
addMouseListener(new MyMouseAdapter(this)); addMouseMotionListener(new
MyMouseMotionAdapter(this));
}
}
class MyMouseAdapter extends MouseAdapter {
AdapterDemo adapterDemo;
public MyMouseAdapter(AdapterDemo adapterDemo) { this.adapterDemo = adapterDemo;
}
// Handle mouse clicked.
public void mouseClicked(MouseEvent me) { adapterDemo.showStatus("Mouse clicked");
}
}
class MyMouseMotionAdapter extends MouseMotionAdapter { AdapterDemo
adapterDemo;
public MyMouseMotionAdapter(AdapterDemo adapterDemo) { this.adapterDemo =
adapterDemo;
}
// Handle mouse dragged.
public void mouseDragged(MouseEvent me) { adapterDemo.showStatus("Mouse
dragged");
}
}
```

Inner Classes: An inner class is a class defined within another class, or even within an expression. This section illustrates how inner classes can be used to simplify the code when using event adapter classes.

To understand the benefit provided by inner classes, consider the applet shown in the following listing. It does not use an inner class. Its goal is to display the string "Mouse Pressed" in the status bar of the applet viewer or browser when the mouse is pressed. There are two top-level classes in this program. **MousePressedDemo** extends **Applet**, and **MyMouseAdapter** extends **MouseAdapter**. The **init( )** method of **MousePressedDemo** instantiates

MyMouseAdapter and provides this object as an argument to the **addMouseListener( )** method.

Notice that a reference to the applet is supplied as an argument to the **MyMouseAdapter** constructor. This reference is stored in an instance variable for later use by the **mousePressed( )** method. When the mouse is pressed, it invokes the **showStatus( )** method of the applet through the stored applet reference. In other words, **showStatus( )** is invoked relative to the applet reference stored by **MyMouseAdapter**.

```
// This applet does NOT use an inner class.
import java.applet.*;
import
java.awt.event.*; /*
   <applet code="MousePressedDemo" width=200
   height=100> </applet>
*/
public class MousePressedDemo extends
   Applet { public void init() {
      addMouseListener(new MyMouseAdapter(this));
   }
}
class MyMouseAdapter extends
   MouseAdapter { MousePressedDemo
   mousePressedDemo;
   public MyMouseAdapter(MousePressedDemo
      mousePressedDemo) { this.mousePressedDemo =
      mousePressedDemo;
   }
   public void mousePressed(MouseEvent me) {
      mousePressedDemo.showStatus("Mouse
```

```
    Pressed.");
  }
}
```

Anonymous Inner Classes: An anonymous inner class is one that is not assigned a name. This section illustrates how an anonymous inner class can facilitate the writing of event handlers. Consider the applet shown in the following listing. As before, its goal is to display the string "Mouse Pressed" in the status bar of the applet viewer or browser when the mouse is pressed.

```
// Anonymous inner class demo. import java.applet.*;
import java.awt.event.*;
/*
 <applet code="AnonymousInnerClassDemo"
   width=200 height=100>
 </applet>
*/
public class AnonymousInnerClassDemo extends Applet
{
 public void init()
  {
   addMouseListener(new MouseAdapter()
   {
    public void mousePressed(MouseEvent me)
     {
      showStatus("Mouse Pressed");
     }
   });
  }
}
```

3.19. Summary

A thread is a single line of execution within a program. Multiple threads can run concurrently in a single program. A thread is created either by subclassing the Thread class or implementing the Runnable interface. We have discussed both the approaches in detail in the chapter. We have also learned the following in the chapter. How to synchronize threads, how to set priorities for threads and how to control the execution of threads. Careful of multithreading will considerably improve the execution speed of Java Programs. A good program does not produce unexpected results. We should incorporate features that could check for potential problems spots in program and guard against program failures. The problem conditions know as exceptions in java must be handled carefully to avoid any program failures and also we learnt what are exceptions how to throw system exceptions and how to define our own exceptions and handle different types of exceptions, where to use the exception tools.

3.20. Questions

1. What is a thread?
2. What is different between multithreading and multitasking? What is to be done to implement these in a program?
3. What java interface must be implemented by all threads?
4. How do we start a thread?
5. What are the two methods by which we may stop threads?
6. What is the difference between suspending and stopping threads?
7. How do we set thread priorities for threads?
8. Describe the life cycle of threads?
9. What is synchronization? When do we use it?
10. Develop a simple real-life application program to illustrate the use of multithreads.

UNIT-4

SWINGS

4.1. Objective

After Going through This Unit, You Should Be Able To

- Understand the components of swing.
- Understand the swing package.
- Create small swing application.
- Understand the basic components of swing and applet.
- Design application using the application using the swing components.

4.2. The Origins of Swing

Swing did not exist in the early days of Java. The AWT defines a basic set of controls, windows, and dialog boxes that support a usable, but limited graphical interface.

One reason for the limited nature of the AWT is that it translates its various visual components into their corresponding, platform-specific equivalents, or peers. This means that the look and feel of a component is defined by the platform, not by Java. Because the AWT components use native code resources, they are referred to as heavyweight.

The use of native peers led to several problems. First, because of variations between operating systems, a component might look, or even act, differently on different platforms.

This potential variability threatened the overarching philosophy of Java: write once, run anywhere. Second, the look and feel of each component was fixed (because it is defined by the platform) and could not be (easily) changed. Third, the use of heavyweight components caused some frustrating restrictions. For example, a heavyweight component is always rectangular and opaque.

Not long after Java's original release, it became apparent that the limitations and restrictions present in the AWT were sufficiently serious that a better approach was needed. The solution was Swing.

Introduced in 1997, Swing was included as part of the Java Foundation Classes (JFC). Swing was initially available for use with Java 1.1 as a separate library. However, beginning with Java 1.2, Swing (and the rest of the JFC) was fully integrated into Java.

4.3. Two Key Swing Features

The two key features: lightweight components and a pluggable look and feel.

Together they provide an elegant, yet easy-to-use solution to the problems of the AWT.

Swing Components Are Lightweight: With very few exceptions, Swing components are lightweight. That is they are written entirely in Java and do not map directly to platform-specific peers. Since lightweight components are rendered using graphics primitives, they can be transparent, which enables nonrectangular shapes. Thus, lightweight components are more efficient and more flexible. Furthermore, because lightweight components do not translate into native peers, the look and feel of each component is determined by Swing, not by the underlying operating system. That is each component will work in a consistent manner across all platforms.

Swing Supports a Pluggable Look and Feel: Swing supports a *pluggable look and feel* (PLAF). Because each Swing component is rendered by Java code rather than by native peers, the look and feel of a component is under the control of Swing. This fact means that it is possible to separate the look and feel of a component from the logic of the component, and this is what Swing does. Separating out the look and feel provides a significant advantage: it becomes possible to change the way that a component is rendered without affecting any of its other aspects. In other words, it is possible to "plug in" a new look and feel for any given component without creating any side effects in the code that uses that component. Moreover, it becomes possible to define entire sets of look-and-feels that represent different GUI styles. To use a specific style, its look and feel is simply "plugged in." Once this is done, all components are automatically rendered using that style.

Pluggable Look-and-Feels Offer Several Important Advantages

It is possible to define a look and feel that is consistent across all platforms.

It is possible to create a look and feel that acts like a specific platform.

Java SE 6 provides look-and-feels, such as metal and Motif, that are available to all Swing users. The metal look and feel is also called the *Java look and feel.*

It is platform-independent and available in all Java execution environments. It is also the default look and feel.

Windows environments also have access to the Windows and Windows Classic look and feel.

4.4. Components and Containers

A Swing GUI consists of two key items: *components* and *containers*. The difference between the two is found in their intended purpose: As the term is commonly used, a *component* is an independent visual control, such as a push button or slider. A container holds a group of components. Thus, a container is a special type of component that is designed to hold other components. Furthermore, in order for a component to be displayed, it must be held within a container. Thus, all Swing GUIs will have at least one container. Because containers are components, a container can also hold other containers. This enables Swing to define what is called a *containment hierarchy*, at the top of which must be a *top-level container*.

Components: In general, Swing components are derived from the **JComponent** class.

JComponent provides the functionality that is common to all components.

For Example

JComponent supports the pluggable look and feel.

JComponent inherits the AWT classes **Container** and **Component**.

Thus, a Swing component is built on and compatible with an AWT component.

All of Swing's components are represented by classes defined within the package **javax.swing**. The following table shows the class names for Swing components (including those used as containers).

JApplet	JButton	JCheckBox	JCheckBoxMenuItem
JColorChooser	JComboBox	JComponent	JDesktopPane
JDialog	JEditorPane	JFileChooser	JFormattedTextField
JFrame	JInternalFrame	JLabel	JLayeredPane
JList	JMenu	JMenuBar	JMenuItem
JOptionPane	JPanel	JPasswordField	JPopupMenu
JProgressBar	JRadioButton	JRadioButtonMenuItem	JRootPane
JScrollBar	JScrollPane	JSeparator	JSlider
JSpinner	JSplitPane	JTabbedPane	JTable
JTextArea	JTextField	JTextPane	JTogglebutton
JToolBar	JToolTip	JTree	JViewport
JWindow			

All component classes begin with the letter **J**. For example, the class for a label is **JLabel**; the class for a push button is **JButton**; and the class for a scroll bar is **JScrollBar**.

Containers: Swing defines two types of containers.

The first are top-level containers: **JFrame**, **JApplet**, **JWindow**, and **JDialog**.

- These containers do not inherit **JComponent.**
- They do, however, inherit the AWT classes **Component** and **Container.**
- Unlike Swing's other components, which are lightweight, the top-level containers are heavyweight.
- As the name implies, a top-level container must be at the top of a containment hierarchy.
- A top-level container is not contained within any other container.
- Every Containment hierarchy must begin with a top-level container.
- The one most commonly used for applications is **JFrame.**
- The one used for applets is **JApplet.**

The second types of containers supported by Swing are lightweight containers. Lightweight containers *do* inherit **JComponent**. An example of a lightweight container is **JPanel**, whichis a general-purpose container.

Lightweight containers are often used to organize and manage groups of related components because a lightweight container can be contained within another container. Thus, you can use lightweight containers such as **JPanel** to create subgroups of related controls that are contained within an outer container.

The Top-Level Container Panes: Each top-level container defines a set of *panes*. At the top of the hierarchy is an instance of **JRootPane**. **JRootPane** is a lightweight container whose purpose is to manage the other panes.

It also helps manage the optional menu bar. The panes that comprise the root pane

are called the *glass pane,* the *content pane,* and the *layered pane.*

The glass pane is the top-level pane. It sits above and completely covers all other panes.

By default, it is a transparent instance of **JPanel**. The glass pane enables you to manage mouse events that affect the entire container (rather than an individual control) or to paint over any other component, for example. In most cases, you won't need to use the glass pane directly, but it is there if you need it. The layered pane is an instance of **JLayeredPane**. The layered pane allows components to be given a depth value. This value determines which component overlays another. (Thus, the layered pane lets you specify a Z-order for a component, although this is not something that you will usually need to do.) The layered pane holds the content pane and the (optional) menu bar. Although the glass pane and the layered panes are integral to the operation of a top-level container and serve important purposes, much of what they provide occurs behind the scene. The pane with which your application will interact the most is the content pane, because this is the pane to which you will add visual components. In other words, when you add a component, such as a button, to a top-level container, you will add it to the content pane. By default, the content pane is an opaque instance of **JPanel**.

4.5. The Swing Packages

Swing is a very large subsystem and makes use of many packages. Following are the packages used by Swing.

javax.swing	javax.swing.border	javax.swing.colorchooser
javax.swing.event	javax.swing.filechooser	javax.swing.plaf
javax.swing.plaf.basic	javax.swing.plaf.metal	javax.swing.plaf.multi
javax.swing.plaf.synth	javax.swing.table	javax.swing.text
javax.swing.text.html	javax.swing.text.html.parser	javax.swing.text.rtf
javax.swing.tree	javax.swing.undo	

The main package is **javax.swing**. This package must be imported into any program that uses Swing. It contains the classes that implement the basic Swing components, such as push buttons, labels, and check boxes.

4.6. A Simple Swing Application

```
// A simple Swing application.
import javax.swing.*;
class SwingDemo {
SwingDemo() {
// Create a new JFrame container.
JFrame jfrm = new JFrame("A Simple Swing Application");
// Give the frame an initial size.
jfrm.setSize(275, 100);
// Terminate the program when the user closes the application.
jfrm.setDefaultCloseOperation(JFrame.EXIT_ON_CLOSE);
// Create a text-based label.
JLabel jlab = new JLabel(" Swing means powerful GUIs.");
// Add the label to the content pane.
jfrm.add(jlab);
// Display the frame.
jfrm.setVisible(true);
```

```
}
public static void main(String args[]) {
// Create the frame on the event dispatching thread.
SwingUtilities.invokeLater(new Runnable() {
public void run() {
new SwingDemo();
}
});
}
}
```

Swing programs are compiled and run in the same way as other Java applications. Thus, to compile this program, you can use this command line:

```
javac SwingDemo.java
```

To run the program, use this command line:

```
java SwingDemo
```

4.7. Create a Swing Applet

Swing-based applets are similar to AWT-based applets, but with an important difference: A Swing applet extends **JApplet** rather than **Applet**. **JApplet** is derived from **Applet**. Thus, **JApplet** includes all of the functionality found in **Applet** and adds support for Swing.

JApplet is a top-level Swing container, which means that it is *not* derived from **JComponent**. Because **JApplet** is a top-level container, it includes the various panes. This means that all components are added to **JApplet**'s content pane in the same way that components are added to **JFrame**'s content pane. Swing applets use the same four lifecycle methods **init( )**,**start( )**, **stop( )**, and **destroy( )**. Of course, you need override only those methods that are needed by your applet. Painting is accomplished differently in Swing than it is in the AWT, and a Swing applet will not normally override the **paint( )** method.

One other point: All interaction with components in a Swing applet must take place on the event dispatching thread, as described in the previous section. This threading issue applies to all Swing programs.

Create a swing applet that has two buttons named alpha and beta. When either of the buttons pressed it should display "alpha was pressed" and "beta was pressed", respectively.

```
// A simple Swing-based applet
```

```
import javax.swing.*;
import java.awt.*;
import java.awt.event.*;
/*
This HTML can be used to launch the applet:
<object code="MySwingApplet" width=220 height=90>
</object>
*/
public class MySwingApplet extends JApplet {
JButton jbtnAlpha;
JButton jbtnBeta;
JLabel jlab;
// Initialize the applet.
public void init() {
try {
SwingUtilities.invokeAndWait(new Runnable () {
public void run() {
makeGUI(); // initialize the GUI
}
});
} catch(Exception exc) {
System.out.println("Can't create because of "+ exc);
}
}
// This applet does not need to override start(), stop(),
// or destroy().
// Set up and initialize the GUI.
private void makeGUI() {
// Set the applet to use flow layout.
setLayout(new FlowLayout());
// Make two buttons.
jbtnAlpha = new JButton("Alpha");
jbtnBeta = new JButton("Beta");
// Add action listener for Alpha.
```

```
jbtnAlpha.addActionListener(new ActionListener() {
public void actionPerformed(ActionEvent le) {
jlab.setText("Alpha was pressed.");
}
});
// Add action listener for Beta.
jbtnBeta.addActionListener(new ActionListener() {
public void actionPerformed(ActionEvent le) {
jlab.setText("Beta was pressed.");
}
});
// Add the buttons to the content pane.
add(jbtnAlpha);
add(jbtnBeta);
// Create a text-based label.
jlab = new JLabel("Press a button.");
// Add the label to the content pane.
add(jlab);
}
}
```

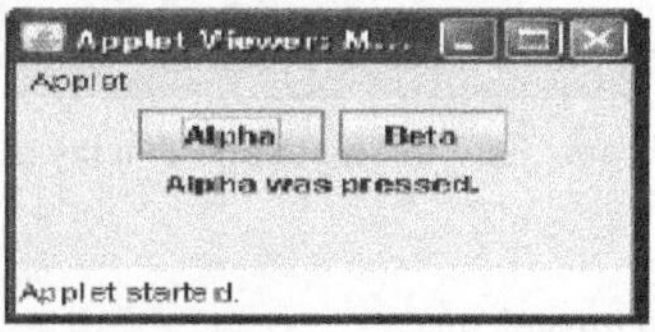

4.8. Jlabel and Imageicon

JLabel is the easiest-to-use component in Swing. It creates a Label. **JLabel** can be used to display text and/or an icon. It is a passive component in that it does not respond to user input.

JLabel defines several constructors. Here are three of them:

JLabel(Icon *icon*)

JLabel(String *str*)

JLabel(String *str*, Icon *icon*, int *align*)

str and icon are the text and icon used for the label. The align argument specifies the horizontal alignment of the text and/or icon within the dimensions of the label. It must be one of the following values: **LEFT**, **RIGHT**, **CENTER**, **LEADING**, or **TRAILING**. These constants are defined in the **SwingConstants** interface, along with several others used by the Swing classes.

Icons are specified by objects of type **Icon**, which is an interface defined by Swing. The easiest way to obtain an icon is to use the **ImageIcon** class. **ImageIcon** implements **Icon** and encapsulates an image. Thus, an object of type **ImageIcon** can be passed as an argument to the **Icon** parameter of **JLabel**'s constructor. There are several ways to provide the image, including reading it from a file or downloading it from a URL. Here is the **ImageIcon** constructor used by the example in this section:

ImageIcon(String *filename*)

It obtains the image in the file named *filename.*

The icon and text associated with the label can be obtained by the following methods:

```
Icon getIcon( )
String getText( )
```

The icon and text associated with a label can be set by these methods:

```
void setIcon(Icon icon)
void setText(String str)
```

Here, icon and str are the icon and text, respectively. Therefore, using **setText( )** it is possible to change the text inside a label during program execution.

The following applet illustrates how to create and display a label containing both an icon and a string.

```
// Demonstrate JLabel and ImageIcon.
import java.awt.*;
import javax.swing.*;
/*
<applet code="JLabelDemo" width=250 height=150>
</applet>
*/
public class JLabelDemo extends JApplet {
public void init() {
try {
```

```
SwingUtilities.invokeAndWait(
new Runnable() {
public void run() {
makeGUI();
}
});
} catch (Exception exc) {
System.out.println("Can't create because of " + exc);
}
}
private void makeGUI() {
// Create an icon.
ImageIcon ii = new ImageIcon("france.gif");
// Create a label.
JLabel jl = new JLabel("France", ii, JLabel.CENTER);
// Add the label to the content pane.
add(jl);
}
}
```

Output from the label example is shown here:

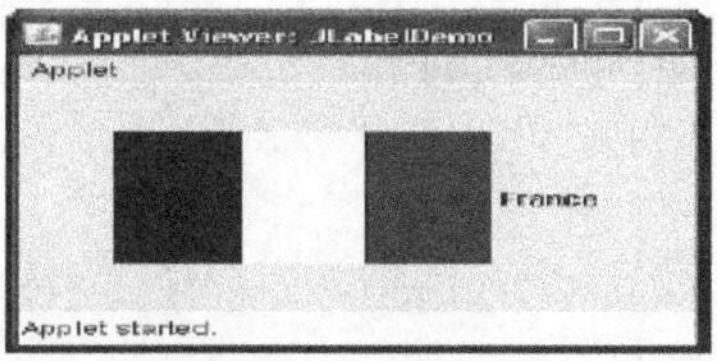

4.9. Jtextfield

JTextField is the simplest Swing text component. It is most widely used text component. **JTextField** allows you to edit one line of text. It is derived from **JTextComponent**, which provides the basic functionality common to Swing text components. **JTextField** uses the **Document** interface for its model. Three of **JTextField**'s constructors are shown here:

JTextField(int *cols*)

JTextField(String *str*, int *cols*)

JTextField(String *str*)

Here, *str* is the string to be initially presented, and *cols* is the number of columns in the text field. If no string is specified, the text field is initially empty. If the number of columns is not specified, the text field is sized to fit the specified string.

JTextField generates events in response to user interaction. For example, an **ActionEvent** is fired when the user presses ENTER. A **CaretEvent** is fired each time the caret (i.e., the cursor) changes position. (**CaretEvent** is packaged in **javax.swing.event.**) Other events are also possible. In many cases, your program will not need to handle these events. Instead, you will simply obtain the string currently in the text field when it is needed. To obtain the text currently in the text field, call **getText( ).**

The following example illustrates **JTextField**. It creates a **JTextField** and adds it to the content pane. When the user presses ENTER, an action event is generated. This is handled by displaying the text in the status window.

```
// Demonstrate JTextField.
    import java.awt.*;
    import java.awt.event.*;
    import javax.swing.*;
    /*
    <applet code="JTextFieldDemo" width=300 height=50>
    </applet>
    */
    public class JTextFieldDemo extends JApplet {
    JTextField jtf;
    public void init() {
    try {
    SwingUtilities.invokeAndWait(
    new Runnable() {
    public void run() {
    makeGUI();
    }
    }
    );
    } catch (Exception exc) {
    System.out.println("Can't create because of " + exc);
    }
```

```
}
private void makeGUI() {
// Change to flow layout.
setLayout(new FlowLayout());
// Add text field to content pane.
jtf = new JTextField(15);
add(jtf);
jtf.addActionListener(new ActionListener() {
public void actionPerformed(ActionEvent ae) {
// Show text when user presses ENTER.
showStatus(jtf.getText());
}
});
}
}
```

Output

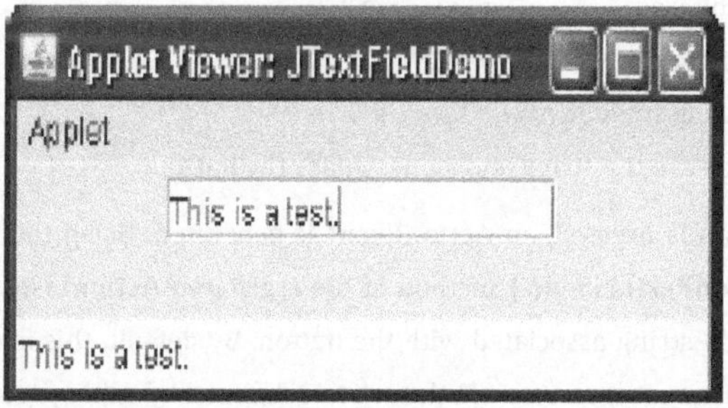

4.10. The Swing Buttons

Swing defines four types of buttons: **JButton**, **JToggleButton**, **JCheckBox**, and **JRadioButton**. All are subclasses of the **AbstractButton** class, which extends **JComponent**. Thus, all buttons share a set of common traits.

AbstractButton contains many methods that allow you to control the behavior of buttons. For example, you can define different icons that are displayed for the button when it is disabled, pressed, or selected. Another icon can be used as a *rollover* icon, which is displayed when the mouse is positioned over a button.

The following methods set these icons:

void setDisabledIcon(Icon *di*)

void setPressedIcon(Icon *pi*)

void setSelectedIcon(Icon *si*)

void setRolloverIcon(Icon *ri*)

Here, *di, pi, si,* and *ri* are the icons to be used for the indicated purpose.

The text associated with a button can be read and written via the following methods:

String getText( )

void setText(String *str*)

Here, *str* is the text to be associated with the button.

The model used by all buttons is defined by the **ButtonModel** interface. A button generates an action event when it is pressed. Other events are possible.

JButton

The **JButton** class provides the functionality of a push button. **JButton** allows an icon, a string, or both to be associated with the push button. Three of its constructors are shown here:

JButton(Icon *icon*)

JButton(String *str*)

JButton(String *str*, Icon *icon*)

Here, *str* and *icon* are the string and icon used for the button.

When the button is pressed, an **ActionEvent** is generated. Using the **ActionEvent** object passed to the **actionPerformed( )** method of the registered **ActionListener**, you can obtain the *action command* string associated with the button. By default, this is the string displayed inside the button. However, you can set the action command by calling **setActionCommand( )** on the button. You can obtain the action command by calling **getActionCommand( )** on the event object. It is declared like this:

String getActionCommand( )

The action command identifies the button. Thus, when using two or more buttons within the same application, the action command gives you an easy way to determine which button was pressed.

The following demonstrates an icon-based button. It displays four push buttons and a label. Each button displays an icon that represents the flag of a country. When a button is pressed, the name of that country is displayed in the label.

```
// Demonstrate an icon-based JButton.
import java.awt.*;
import java.awt.event.*;
import javax.swing.*;
/*
<applet code="JButtonDemo" width=250 height=450>
</applet>
*/
public class JButtonDemo extends JApplet
implements ActionListener {
JLabel jlab;
public void init() {
try {
SwingUtilities.invokeAndWait(
new Runnable() {
public void run() {
makeGUI();
}
}
);
} catch (Exception exc) {
System.out.println("Can't create because of " + exc);
}
}
private void makeGUI() {
// Change to flow layout.
setLayout(new FlowLayout());
// Add buttons to content pane.
ImageIcon france = new ImageIcon("france.gif");
JButton jb = new JButton(france);
jb.setActionCommand("France");
jb.addActionListener(this);
add(jb);
ImageIcon germany = new ImageIcon("germany.gif");
```

```
jb = new JButton(germany);
jb.setActionCommand("Germany");
jb.addActionListener(this);
add(jb);
ImageIcon italy = new ImageIcon("italy.gif");
jb = new JButton(italy);
jb.setActionCommand("Italy");
jb.addActionListener(this);
add(jb);
ImageIcon japan = new ImageIcon("japan.gif");
jb = new JButton(japan);
jb.setActionCommand("Japan");
jb.addActionListener(this);
add(jb);
// Create and add the label to content pane.
jlab = new JLabel("Choose a Flag");
add(jlab);
}
// Handle button events.
public void actionPerformed(ActionEvent ae) {
jlab.setText("You selected " + ae.getActionCommand());
}
}
```

Output

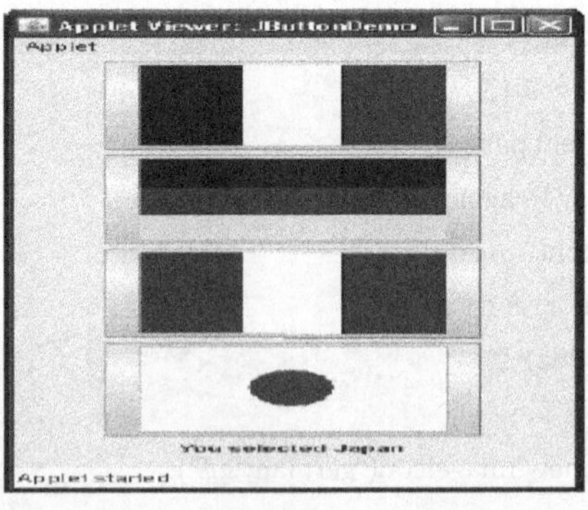

4.11. Jtabbedpane

JTabbedPane encapsulates a *tabbed pane*. It manages a set of components by linking them with tabs. Selecting a tab causes the component associated with that tab to come to the forefront.

JTabbedPane defines three constructors. Here we will use its default constructor, which creates an empty control with the tabs positioned across the top of the pane. The other two constructors let you specify the location of the tabs, which can be along any of the four sides. JTabbedPane uses the SingleSelectionModel model. Tabs are added by calling addTab( ). Here is one of its forms:

void addTab(String name, Component comp)

Here, name is the name for the tab, and comp is the component that should be added to the tab. Often, the component added to a tab is a JPanel that contains a group of related components. This technique allows a tab to hold a set of components.

The general procedure to use a tabbed pane is outlined here:

1. Create an instance of **JTabbedPane**.
2. Add each tab by calling **addTab( )**.
3. Add the tabbed pane to the content pane.

The following example illustrates a tabbed pane. The first tab is titled "Cities" and contains four buttons. Each button displays the name of a city. The second tab is titled "Colors" and contains three check boxes. Each check box displays the name of a color. The third tab is titled "Flavors" and contains one combo box. This enables the user to select one of three flavors.

```
// Demonstrate JTabbedPane.
import javax.swing.*;
/*
<applet code="JTabbedPaneDemo" width=400 height=100>
</applet>
*/
public class JTabbedPaneDemo extends JApplet {
public void init() {
try {
SwingUtilities.invokeAndWait(
new Runnable() {
public void run() {
```

```
makeGUI();
}
}
);
} catch (Exception exc) {
System.out.println("Can't create because of " + exc);
}
}
private void makeGUI() {
JTabbedPane jtp = new JTabbedPane();
jtp.addTab("Cities", new CitiesPanel());
jtp.addTab("Colors", new ColorsPanel());
jtp.addTab("Flavors", new FlavorsPanel());
add(jtp);
}
}
// Make the panels that will be added to the tabbed pane.
class CitiesPanel extends JPanel {
public CitiesPanel() {
JButton b1 = new JButton("New York");
add(b1);
JButton b2 = new JButton("London");
add(b2);
JButton b3 = new JButton("Hong Kong");
add(b3);
JButton b4 = new JButton("Tokyo");
add(b4);
}
}
class ColorsPanel extends JPanel {
public ColorsPanel() {
JCheckBox cb1 = new JCheckBox("Red");
add(cb1);
JCheckBox cb2 = new JCheckBox("Green");
```

```
add(cb2);
JCheckBox cb3 = new JCheckBox("Blue");
add(cb3);
}
}
class FlavorsPanel extends JPanel {
public FlavorsPanel() {
JComboBox jcb = new JComboBox();
jcb.addItem("Vanilla");
jcb.addItem("Chocolate");
jcb.addItem("Strawberry");
add(jcb);
}
}
```

Output from the tabbed pane example is shown in the following three illustrations:

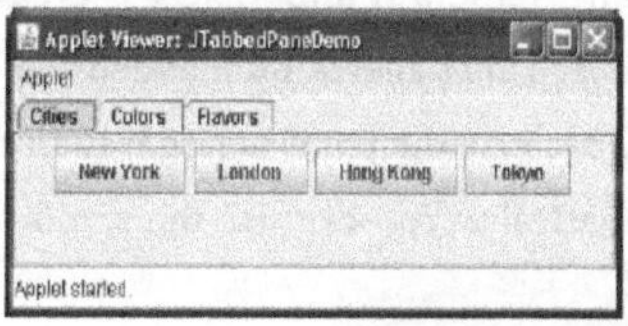

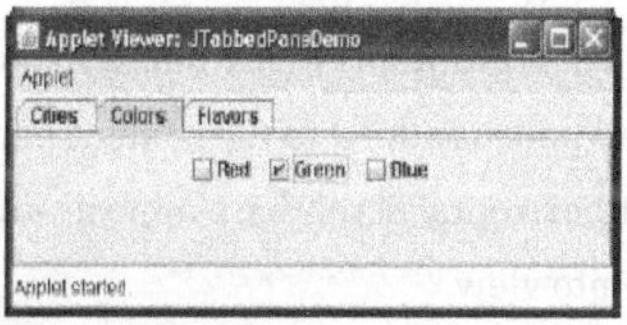

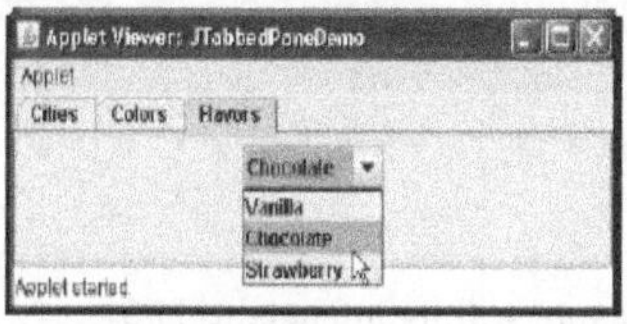

4.12. Jscrollpane

JScrollPane is a lightweight container that automatically handles the scrolling of another component. The component being scrolled can either be an individual component, such as a table, or a group of components contained within another lightweight container, such as a **JPanel**. In either case, if the object being scrolled is larger than the viewable area, horizontal and/or vertical scroll bars are automatically provided, and the component can be scrolled through the pane. Because **JScrollPane** automates scrolling, it usually eliminates the need to manage individual scroll bars.

The viewable area of a scroll pane is called the *viewport*. It is a window in which the component being scrolled is displayed. Thus, the viewport displays the visible portion of the component being scrolled. The scroll bars scroll the component through the viewport. In its default behavior, a **JScrollPane** will dynamically add or remove a scroll bar as needed. For example, if the component is taller than the viewport, a vertical scroll bar is added. If the component will completely fit within the viewport, the scroll bars are removed.

JScrollPane defines several constructors.

JScrollPane(Component *comp*)

The component to be scrolled is specified by *comp*. Scroll bars are automatically displayed when the content of the pane exceeds the dimensions of the viewport.

Here are the steps to follow to use a scroll pane:

1. Create the component to be scrolled.
2. Create an instance of **JScrollPane**, passing to it the object to scroll.
3. Add the scroll pane to the content pane.

The following example illustrates a scroll pane. First, a **JPanel** object is created, and 400 buttons are added to it, arranged into 20 columns. This panel is then added to a scroll pane, and the scroll pane is added to the content pane. Because the panel is larger than the viewport, vertical and horizontal scroll bars appear automatically. You can use the scroll bars to scroll the buttons into view.

```
// Demonstrate JScrollPane.
import java.awt.*;
import javax.swing.*;
/*
<applet code="JScrollPaneDemo" width=300 height=250>
</applet>
*/
public class JScrollPaneDemo extends JApplet {
public void init() {
try {
SwingUtilities.invokeAndWait(
new Runnable() {
public void run() {
makeGUI();
}
```

```
}
);
} catch (Exception exc) {
System.out.println("Can't create because of " + exc);
}
}
private void makeGUI() {
// Add 400 buttons to a panel.
JPanel jp = new JPanel();
jp.setLayout(new GridLayout(20, 20));
int b = 0;
for(int i = 0; i < 20; i++) {
for(int j = 0; j < 20; j++) {
jp.add(new JButton("Button " + b));
++b;
}
}
// Create the scroll pane.
JScrollPane jsp = new JScrollPane(jp);
// Add the scroll pane to the content pane.
// Because the default border layout is used,
// the scroll pane will be added to the center.
add(jsp, BorderLayout.CENTER);
}
}
```

Output from the scroll pane example is shown here:

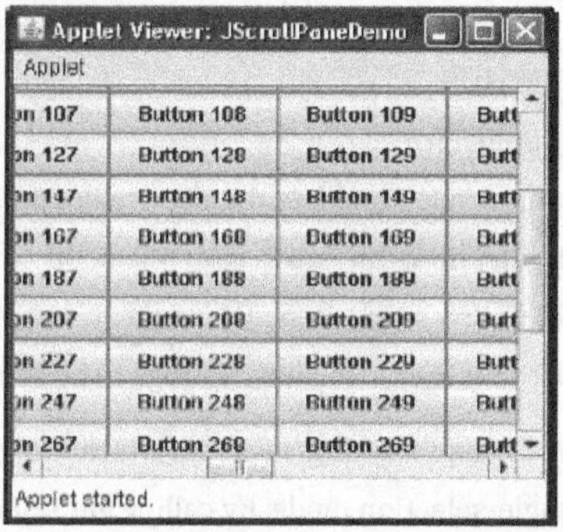

4.13. Jlist

In Swing, the basic list class is called **JList**. It supports the selection of one or more items from a list. **JList** provides several constructors. The one used here is

JList(Object[ ] *items*)

This creates a **JList** that contains the items in the array specified by *items*. **JList** is based on two models. The first is **ListModel**. This interface defines how access to the list data is achieved. The second model is the **ListSelectionModel** interface, which defines methods that determine what list item or items are selected.

A**JList** generates a **ListSelectionEvent** when the user makes or changes a selection.

This event is also generated when the user deselects an item. It is handled by implementing **ListSelectionListener**. This listener specifies only one method, called **valueChanged( )**, which is shown here:

void valueChanged(ListSelectionEvent *le*)

Here, *le* is a reference to the object that generated the event. Although **ListSelectionEvent** does provide some methods of its own, normally you will interrogate the **JList** object itself to determine what has occurred. Both **ListSelectionEvent** and **ListSelectionListener** are packaged in **javax.swing.event**.

By default, a **JList** allows the user to select multiple ranges of items within the list, but you can change this behavior by calling **setSelectionMode( )**, which is defined by **JList**. It is shown here:

void setSelectionMode(int *mode*)

Here, *mode* specifies the selection mode. It must be one of these values defined by

ListSelectionModel

SINGLE_SELECTION
SINGLE_INTERVAL_SELECTION
MULTIPLE_INTERVAL_SELECTION

The default, multiple-interval selection, lets the user select multiple ranges of items within a list. With single-interval selection, the user can select one range of items. With single selection, the user can select only a single item. Of course, a single item can be selected in the other two modes, too. It's just that they also allow a range to be selected.

You can obtain the index of the first item selected, which will also be the index of the only selected item when using single-selection mode, by calling **getSelectedIndex( )**, shown here:

```
int getSelectedIndex( )
```

Indexing begins at zero. So, if the first item is selected, this method will return 0. If no item is selected, –1 is returned.

Instead of obtaining the index of a selection, you can obtain the value associated with the selection by calling **getSelectedValue( )**:

```
Object getSelectedValue( )
```

It returns a reference to the first selected value. If no value has been selected, it returns **null**. The following applet demonstrates a simple **JList**, which holds a list of cities. Each time a city is selected in the list, a **ListSelectionEvent** is generated, which is handled by the **valueChanged( )** method defined by **ListSelectionListener**. It responds by obtaining the index of the selected item and displaying the name of the selected city in a label.

```
// Demonstrate JList.
import javax.swing.*;
import javax.swing.event.*;
import java.awt.*;
import java.awt.event.*;
/*
<applet code="JListDemo" width=200 height=120>
</applet>
*/
public class JListDemo extends JApplet {
JList jlst;
JLabel jlab;
JScrollPane jscrlp;
// Create an array of cities.
String Cities[] = { "New York", "Chicago", "Houston",
"Denver", "Los Angeles", "Seattle",
"London", "Paris", "New Delhi",
"Hong Kong", "Tokyo", "Sydney" };
public void init() {
try {
SwingUtilities.invokeAndWait(
new Runnable() {
public void run() {
```

```
makeGUI();
}
}
);
} catch (Exception exc) {
System.out.println("Can't create because of " + exc);
}
}
private void makeGUI() {
// Change to flow layout.
setLayout(new FlowLayout());
// Create a JList.
jlst = new JList(Cities);
// Set the list selection mode to single selection.
jlst.setSelectionMode(ListSelectionModel.SINGLE_SELECTION);
// Add the list to a scroll pane.
jscrlp = new JScrollPane(jlst);
// Set the preferred size of the scroll pane.
jscrlp.setPreferredSize(new Dimension(120, 90));
// Make a label that displays the selection.
jlab = new JLabel("Choose a City");
// Add selection listener for the list.
jlst.addListSelectionListener(new ListSelectionListener() {
public void valueChanged(ListSelectionEvent le) {
// Get the index of the changed item.
int idx = jlst.getSelectedIndex();
// Display selection, if item was selected.
if(idx != -1)
jlab.setText("Current selection: " + Cities[idx]);
else // Otherwise, reprompt.
jlab.setText("Choose a City");
}
});
// Add the list and label to the content pane.
```

```
add(jscrlp);
add(jlab);
}
}
```

Output from the list example is shown here:

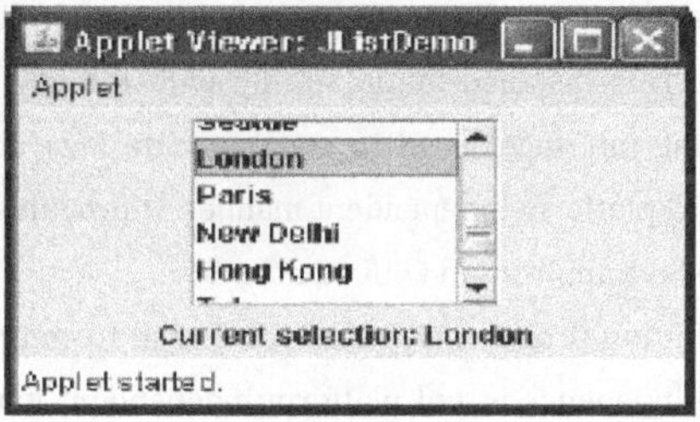

4.14. Questions

1. Discuss about swing feature. List its components and containers.
2. Develop an applet to create a label. a text field and 4 check boxes with the caption "red", "green" ,"blue" and "yellow".
3. What are swings provide any two typical applications of swings?
4. Explain various components of the swing package?
5. Create a swing applet that has two buttons named alpha and beta. When either of the buttons pressed it should display "alpha was pressed" and "beta was pressed", respectively?
6. Name and explain different types of swing Buttons. Give their syntax?
7. Write the steps to create JTable. Write a program to create a table with column headings "Fname, Lname, Age" and insert at least five records in the table and display the records?
8. Explain JScrollPane and JComboBox with a program?
9. Explain the containers and components in swings?
10. Explain with an example for each,
    i). JTextField class ii). JButton class iii). JComboBox class.
11. How AWT is different from swings? What are the two key features of it ? Explain?
12. List four types of buttons in swings with their use. Write a program to create four different types of button on JApplet. Use suitable events to show actions on the buttons and use JLabel to display the action invoked.

UNIT-5

ENTERPRISE EDITION OVERVIEW, DATABASE ACCESS

5.1. Introduction

JDBC (Java Database Connectivity) is uses for connect java application with database. It is Java SE technology, which is installed automatically with the jdk software. Jdbc is an API (Application programming interface) used to communicate Java application to database in database independent and platform independent manner. It provides classes and interfaces to connect or communicate Java application with database.

Jdbc is an API (Application programming interface) used to communicate Java application to database in database independent and platform independent manner. It provides classes and interfaces to connect or communicate Java application with database. Jdbc is a part of JDK software so no needs to install separate software for jdbc API. Jdbc API consists of two packages:

1) java.sql package.
2) javax.sql package.

JDBC API is a Java API that can access any kind of data stored in a Relational Database. It enables Java programs to execute SQL statements. JDBC works with Java on a variety of platforms, such as Windows, Mac OS, and the various versions of UNIX.

5.2. Objective

After learning this chapter students will be able to

Describe and design the database

Explain various types of drivers used for connection to database

Develop the database small projects

Describe the metadata etc

5.3. Overview of J2EE and J2SE

1) Java™2 Platform, Enterprise Edition (J2EE™) technology provides a component-based approach to the design, development, assembly, and deployment of enterprise applications.
2) The J2EE platform gives you a multitier distributed application model, the ability to reuse components, integrated XML-based data interchange, a unified security model, and flexible transaction control.

3) Vendors and customers enjoy the freedom to choose the products and components that best meet their business and technological requirements.

5.4. The Concept of JDBC

There are many industrial-strength DBMSs on the market, including Oracle, DB2, Sybase, and many other popular brands. The challenge faced by Sun Microsystems in the late 1990s was to develop a way for Java developers to write high-level code that accesses all popular DBMSs. One major obstacle to overcome was a language barrier. Each DBMS defined its own low-level way to interact with programs to access data stored in its databases. This meant that low-level code written to communicate with an Oracle database might need to be rewritten to access a DB2 database.

Sun met the challenge in 1996 with the creation of the JDBC driver and the JDBC API. Both were created out of necessity because until then Java couldn't access DBMSs and therefore wasn't considered an industrial-strength programming language. The JDBC driver developed by Sun wasn't a driver at all. It was a specification that described the detailed functionality of a JDBC driver. DBMS manufacturers and third-party vendors were encouraged to build JDBC drivers that conformed to Sun's specifications. Those firms who built JDBC drivers for their products could tap into the growing Java applications market. The specifications required a JDBC driver to be a translator that converts low-level proprietary DBMS messages to low-level messages that are understood by the JDBC API and vice versa. This meant Java programmers could use high-level JDBC interfaces that are defined in the JDBC API to write a routine that interacts with the DBMS. The JDBC interface converts the routine into low-level messages that conform to the JDBC driver specification and sends them to the JDBC driver. The JDBC driver translates the routine into low-level messages that are understood and processed by the DBMS.

5.5. JDBC Driver Types

JDBC Driver is a software component that enables java application to communicate with the database. There are 4 types of JDBC drivers, they are:

1) Jdbc-Odbc Bridge Driver.
2) Native-API driver (partially java driver).
3) Network Protocol driver (fully java driver).
4) Thin driver (fully java driver).

Short Description of JDBC Drivers

1) Type 1 driver is database independent and platform dependent.
2) Type 2 driver are database dependent and platform dependent.

3) Type 3 driver are database independent and platform independent.

4) Type 4 driver are database dependent and platform independent.

Driver	Database	Platform
Type - 1	Independent	Dependent.
Type - 2	Dependent	Dependent.
Type - 3	Independent	Independent.
Type - 4	Dependent	Independent.

JDBC ODBC Bridge Driver

This driver connects a java program with a database using Odbc driver. It is install automatically along with jdk software. It is provided by Sun MicroSystem for testing purpose this driver cannot be used in real time application. This driver convert Jdbc calls into Odbc calls(function) So this is called a **bridge driver**.

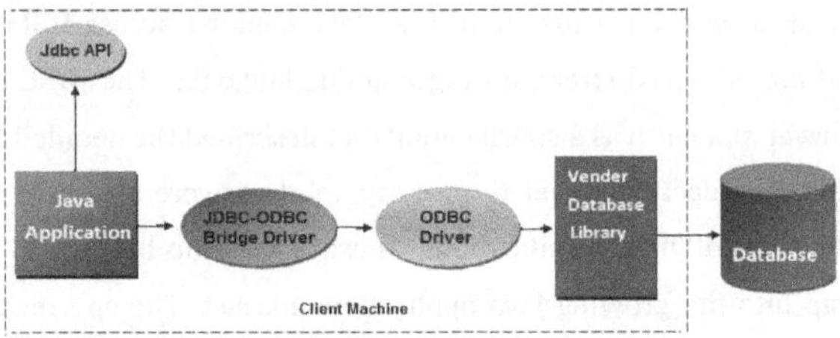

JDBC-ODBC bridge driver

Advantage of Bridge Driver

1) Easy to use
2) It is a database independent driver
3) Can be easily connected to any database.
4) This driver software is built-in with JDK so no need to install separately.

Disadvantage of Bridge Driver

1) It is a slow driver so not used in real time application
2) Because of Odbc connectivity it is a platform dependent driver.
3) It is not a portable driver.
4) It is not suitable for applet to connect with database.

Native API driver

Native API driver uses native API to connect a java program directly to the database. Native API id s C, C++ library, which contains a set of function used to connect with database directly.

Native API will be different from one database to another database. So this Native API driver is a database dependent driver.

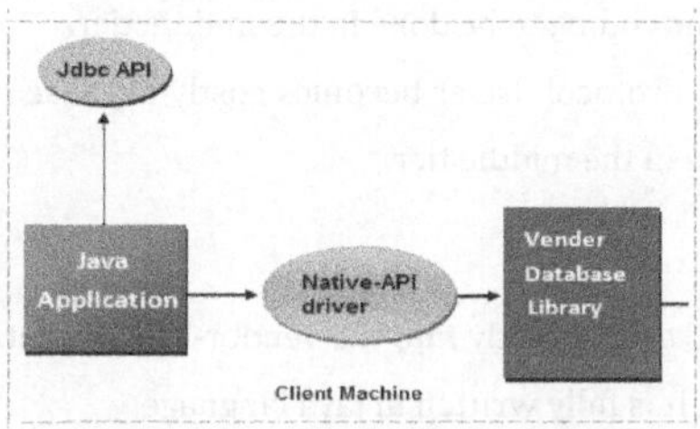

Native-API Driver

Advantage of Thin Driver

1) Native API driver comparatively faster than JDBC-ODBC bridge driver.

Disadvantage of Thin Driver

1) Native API driver is database dependent and also platform dependent because of Native API.

Network Protocol Driver

1) The Network Protocol driver uses middle-ware (application server) that converts JDBC calls directly or indirectly into the vendor-specific database protocol. It is fully written in java.

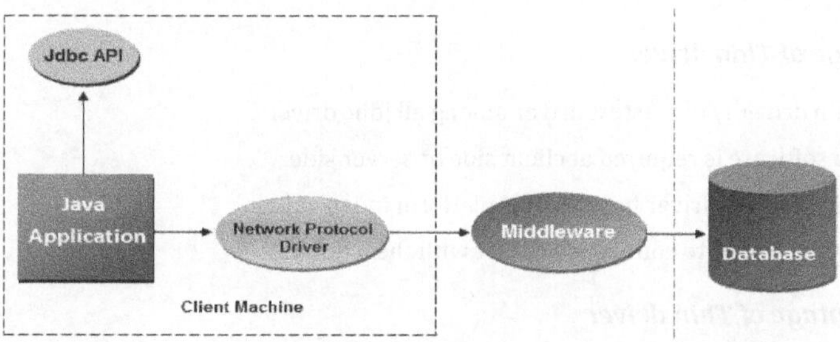

Network Protocol driver

Advantage of Network Protocol Driver

1) No client side library is required because of application server that can perform many tasks like auditing, load balancing, logging etc.
2) This driver is both database and platform independent driver

Disadvantage of Network Protocol Driver

1) Network support is required on client machine.
2) Requires database-specific coding to be done in the middle tier.
3) Maintenance of Network Protocol driver becomes costly because it requires database-specific coding to be done in the middle tier.

Thin Driver

The thin driver converts JDBC calls directly into the vendor-specific database protocol. That is why it is known as thin driver. It is fully written in Java language.

This thin driver uses the following three information to connect with a database.

1) Ip address of a machine (system), where the database server is running.
2) Port number of the database server.
3) Database name, also called SID (service ID).

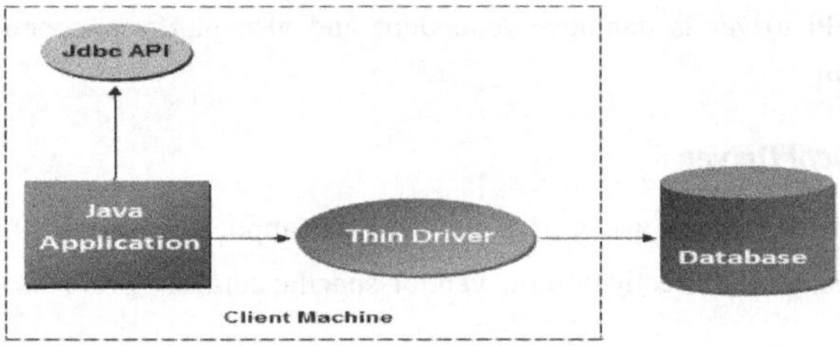

Thin driver

Advantage of Thin driver

1) Thin driver is the fastest driver among all Jdbc drivers.
2) No software is required at client side or server side.
3) It is portable driver because it is platform independent.
4) It can be used to connect an applet with the database.

Disadvantage of Thin driver

1) Thin driver is a database dependent driver.

5.6. JDBC Packages

Jdbc API consists of two packages:

1) java.sql package
2) javax.sql package

5.7. Overview of the JDBC Process

Before you can create a java jdbc connection to the database, you must first import the java.sql package. import java.sql.*; The star (*) indicates that all of the classes in the package java.sql are to be imported.

Java application calls the JDBC library. JDBC loads a driver which talks to the database. We can change database engines without changing database code.

Establishing Database Connection and Associating JDBC/ODBC bridge.

There are 6 steps to connect any java application with the database using JDBC. They are as follows:

1. Load the JDBC driver class or register the JDBC driver.
2. Establish the connection.
3. Create a statement.
4. Execute the sql commands on database and get the result.
5. Print the result.
6. Close the connection.

5.8. Database Connection Associating the JDBC/ODBC Bridge with the Database

You use the ODBC Data Source Administrator to create the association between the database and the JDBC/ODBC Bridge. Here's what you need to do:

1) Select Start | Settings | Control Panel.
2) Select ODBC 32 to display the ODBC Data Source Administrator.
3) Add a new user by selecting the Add button.
4) Select the driver, and then select Finish. Use the Microsoft Access Driver if you are using Microsoft Access, otherwise select the driver for the DBMS that you are using. If you don't find the driver for your DBMS on the list, you'll need to install the driver. Contact the manufacturer of the DBMS for more information on how to obtain the driver.
5) Enter the name of the database as the Data Source name in the ODBC Microsoft Access Setup dialog box. This is the name that will be used within your Java database program to connect to the DBMS.
6) Enter a description for the data source. This is optional, but will be a reminder of the kind of data stored in the database.

7) Click the Select button. You'll be prompted to browse the directory of each hard drive connected to your computer in order to define the direct path to the database. Click OK once you locate the database, and the directory path and name of the database will be displayed in the ODBC Microsoft Access Setup dialog box.
8) Since this is your database, you can determine whether a login name and password are required to access the database. If so, click the Advanced button to display the Set Advanced Options dialog box. This dialog box is used to assign a login name (also referred to as a user ID) and a password to the database. Select OK. If not, skip this step.
9) When the ODBC Microsoft Access Setup dialog box appears, select OK.
10) Select OK to close the ODBC Data Source Administrator dialog box.

5.9. Statement Objects

Once a connection to the database is opened, the J2EE application creates and sends a query to access data contained in the database. The query is written using SQL One of three types of Statement objects is used to **execute** the query. These objects are Statement, which executes a query immediately; **PreparedStatement,** which is used to execute a compiled query **CallableStatement**,which is used to execute store procedures.

```
String url = "jdbc:odbc:CustomerInformation";
String userID = "jim";
String password = "keogh";
Statement DataRequest;
ResultSet Results;
Connection Db;
try {
Class.forName( "sun.jdbc.odbc.JdbcOdbcDriver");
Db = DriverManager.getConnection(url,userID,password);
}
catch (ClassNotFoundException error) {
System.err.println("Unable to load the JDBC/ODBC bridge." +
error);
System.exit(1);
}
catch (SQLException error) {
System.err.println("Cannot connect to the database." + error);
```

```
System.exit(2);
}
try {
String query = "SELECT * FROM Customers";
DataRequest = Db.createStatement();
Results = DataRequest.executeQuery (query);
//Place code here to interact with the ResultSet
DataRequest.close();
}
catch ( SQLException error ){
System.err.println("SQL error." + error);
System.exit(3);
}
Db.close();
```

5.10. Resultset

The Result Set object contains methods that are used to copy data from the ResultSet into a Java collection of objects or variable(s) for further processing. Data in a ResultSet object is logically organized into a virtual table consisting of rows and columns. In addition to data, the ResultSet object also contains metadata, such as column names, column size, and column data type.

The ResultSet uses a virtual cursor to point to a row of the virtual table. A J2EE application must move the virtual cursor to each row, then use other methods of the ResultSet object to interact with the data stored in columns of that row. The virtual cursor is positioned above the first row of data when the ResultSet is returned by the executeQuery() method. This means that the virtual cursor must be moved to the first row using the next() method. The next() method returns a boolean true if the row contains data, otherwise a boolean false is returned, indicating that no more rows exist in the ResultSet.

Once the virtual cursor points to a row, the get*XXX*() method is used to copy data from the row to a collection, object, or variable. the get*XXX*() method is data type specific. For example, the getString() method is used to copy String data from a column of the ResultSet. The data type of the get*XXX*() method must be the same data type of the column in the ResultSet. The get*XXX*() method requires one parameter, which is an integer that represents the number of the column that contains the data. For example, getString(1) copies the data from the first column of the ResultSet.

```
String url = "jdbc:odbc:CustomerInformation";
String userID = "jim";
String password = "keogh";
String printrow;
String FirstName;
String LastName;
Statement DataRequest;
ResultSet Results;
Connection Db;
try {
Class.forName( "sun.jdbc.odbc.JdbcOdbcDriver");
Db = DriverManager.getConnection(url,userID,password);
}
catch (ClassNotFoundException error) {
System.err.println("Unable to load the JDBC/ODBC bridge." +
error);
System.exit(1);
}
catch (SQLException error) {
System.err.println("Cannot connect to the database." + error);
System.exit(2);
}
try {
String query = "SELECT FirstName,LastName FROM Customers";
DataRequest = Db.createStatement();
Results = DataRequest.executeQuery (query);
}
catch ( SQLException error ){
System.err.println("SQL error." + error);
System.exit(3);
}
boolean Records = Results.next();
```

```
if (!Records ) {
System.out.println("No data returned");
System.exit(4);
}
try {
do {
FirstName = Results.getString ( 1 ) ;
LastName = Results.getString ( 2 ) ;
printrow = FirstName + " " + LastName;
System.out.println(printrow);
} while (Results.next() );
DataRequest.close();
}
catch (SQLException error ) {
System.err.println("Data display error." + error);
System.exit(5);
}
```

5.11. Transaction Processing

A transaction may involve several tasks similar to the tasks required to complete a transaction at a supermarket. In a supermarket transaction, each item purchased must be registered, the transaction must be totaled, and the customer must tender the amount of the purchase. The transaction is successfully completed only if each task is completed successfully. If one task fails, the entire transaction fails. Previously completed tasks must be reversed if the transaction fails. For example, goods that were registered must be removed from the register and returned to the shelf.

A database transaction consists of a set of SQL statements, each of which must be successfully completed for the transaction to be completed. If one fails, SQL statements that executed successfully up to that point in the transaction must be rolled back. A database transaction isn't completed until the J2EE application calls the commit() method of the Connection object. All SQL statements executed before the call to the commit() method can be rolled back. However, once the commit() method is called, none of the SQL statements can be rolled back. The commit() method must be called regardless of whether the SQL statement is part of a transaction or not.

If a J2EE application is processing a transaction, the AutoCommit feature must be deactivated by calling the setAutoCommit() method and passing it a false parameter.

Once the transaction is completed, the setAutoCommit() method is called again, this time passing it a true parameter, which reactivates the AutoCommit feature.

5.12. Metadata

Metadata is data about data. A J2EE application can access metadata by using the DatabaseMetaData interface. The DatabaseMetaData interface is used to retrieve information about databases, tables, columns, and indexes, among other information about the DBMS. A J2EE application retrieves metadata about the database by calling the getMetaData() method of the Connection object. The getMetaData() method returns a DatabaseMetaData object that contains information about the database and its components.

Once the DatabaseMetaData object is obtained, an assortment of methods contained in the DatabaseMetaData object are called to retrieve specific metadata. Here are some of the more commonly used DatabaseMetaData object methods:

- **getDatabaseProductName()** Returns the product name of the database.
- **getUserName()** Returns the user name.
- **getURL()** Returns the URL of the database.
- **getSchemas()** Returns all the schema names available in this database.
- **getPrimaryKeys()** Returns primary keys.
- **getProcedures()** Returns stored procedure names.
- **getTables()** Returns names of tables in the database.

5.13. Summary

In this chapter we have learnt the basic of JDBC, JDBC Drivers, how to establish the connection to the jdbc, retrieve the values from jdbc and learnt some method of transaction processing. Resultset, different methods of statement objects.

5.14. Questions

1. Provide various classes interfaces and exceptions available under java sql package, along with their proper syntax?
2. Give the JAVA syntax for the following:
   i. Connecting to a database using JDBC/ODBC bridge, which has url= "jdbc : odbc : SDB", Username = "Scott" and password = "tiger"

ii. Running a query "select emp-age from emp" over that connected database.

iii. Counting number of employees, with the condition emp –age > 50.

3. Explain the J2EE multitier Architecture.
4. Describe the various steps of JDBC, with code snippets.
5. What are the transactions? Explain.
6. Write a note on database metadata interface.
7. What do you ment by scrollable resultset? Explain?
8. Give an overview of the JDBC process?
9. With proper syntax, explain three types of getConnection method().
10. Briefly explain the callable statement object. Write a program to call a stored procedure.
11. What is transaction processing? Write a program to execute a database transaction.
12. Briefly discuss about the various JDBC driver types?.
13. Write program to display the current contents of a table in the database.

UNIT-6

SERVLETS

6.1. Introduction

In order to understand the advantages of servlets, the first and for most is that we must have a basic understanding of how web browsers and servers cooperate to provide content to a user.

Example: Consider a request for a static web page. A user enters a Uniform Resource Locator (URL) into a browser. The browser generates an HTTP request to the appropriate web server. The web server maps this request to a specific file. That file is returned in an HTTP response to the browser. The HTTP header in the response indicates the type of the content. The Multipurpose Internet Mail Extensions (MIME) is used for this purpose.

For example, ordinary ASCII text has a MIME type of text/plain. The Hypertext Markup Language (HTML) source code of a web page has a MIME type of text/html.

Now consider dynamic content. Assume that an online store uses a database to store information about its business. This would include items for sale, prices, availability, orders, and so forth. It wishes to make this information accessible to customers via web pages. The contents of those web pages must be dynamically generated to reflect the latest information in the database.

In the early days of the Web, a server could dynamically construct a page by creating a separate process to handle each client request. The process would open connections to one or more databases in order to obtain the necessary information.

It communicated with the web server via an interface known as the Common Gateway Interface (CGI). CGI allowed the separate process to read data from the HTTP request and write data to the HTTP response.

A variety of different languages were used to build CGI programs. These included C, C++, and Perl. However, CGI suffered serious performance problems. It was expensive in terms of processor and memory resources to create a separate process for each client request. It was also expensive to open and close database connections for each client request. In addition the CGI programs were not platform-independent. Therefore, other techniques were introduced. Among these are servlets. Servlets offer several advantages in comparison with CGI.

- First, performance is significantly better. Servlets execute within the address space of a web server. It is not necessary to create a separate process to handle each client request.
- Second, servlets are platform-independent because they are written in Java.
- Third, the Java security manager on the server enforces a set of restrictions to protect the resources on a server machine.
- Finally, the full functionality of the Java class libraries is available to a servlet. It can communicate with applets, databases, or other software via the sockets and RMI mechanisms.

6.2. Objective

Students will be able to:

Describe the life cycle of servlet

Describe the tomcat server used for servlet development

Develop small servlet applications

Describe the reading the parameters

Describe the session tracking.

6.3. The Life Cycle of a Servlet

Three methods are central to the life cycle of a servlet. These are **init( )**, **service( )**, and **destroy( )**. They are implemented by every servlet and are invoked at specific times by the server. Let us consider a typical user scenario to understand when these methods are called.

- **First,** assume that a user enters a Uniform Resource Locator (URL) to a web browser. The browser then generates an HTTP request for this URL. This request is then sent to the appropriate server.
- **Second,** this HTTP request is received by the web server. The server maps this request to a particular servlet. The servlet is dynamically retrieved and loaded into the address space of the server.
- **Third,** the server invokes the **init( )** method of the servlet. This method is invoked only when the servlet is first loaded into memory. It is possible to pass initialization parameters to the servlet so it may configure itself.
- **Fourth,** the server invokes the **service( )** method of the servlet. This method is called to process the HTTP request. It may also formulate an HTTP response for the client.

- The servlet remains in the server's address space and is available to process any other HTTP requests received from clients. The **service( )** method is called for each HTTP request.
- **Finally,** the server may decide to unload the servlet from its memory. The algorithms by which this determination is made are specific to each server. The server calls the **destroy( )** method to relinquish any resources such as file handles that are allocated for the servlet. Important data may be saved to a persistent store. The memory allocated for the servlet and its objects can then be garbage collected.

6.4. Using Tomcat for Servlet Development

To create servlets, you will need access to a servlet development environment. The one used in this chapter is Tomcat. Tomcat is an open-source product maintained by the Jakarta Project of the Apache Software Foundation. It contains the class libraries, documentation, and runtime support that were we need to create and test servlets.

Here we are using Tomcat 5.5.17. Tomcat is a free open source and it can be downloadable from jakarta.apache.org.

The Default Location for Tomcat 5.5.17 in Windows Environment is C:\Program Files\Apache Software Foundation\Tomcat 5.5\.

If the Tomcat in a different location, we need to make appropriate changes to the examples. We may need to set the environmental variable **JAVA_HOME** to the top-level directory in which the Java Development Kit is installed.

To start Tomcat, select Configure Tomcat in the Start | Programs menu, and then press Start in the Tomcat Properties dialog. When you are done testing servlets, you can stop Tomcat by pressing Stop in the Tomcat Properties dialog.

The directory C:\Program Files\Apache Software Foundation\Tomcat 5.5\common\lib\ contains **servlet-api.jar**. This JAR file contains the classes and interfaces that are needed to build servlets. To make this file accessible, update **CLASSPATH** environment variable so that it includes

C:\Program Files\Apache Software Foundation\Tomcat 5.5\common\lib\servlet-api.jar

Alternatively, you can specify this file when you compile the servlets.

For example, the following command compiles the first servlet example:

javac HelloServlet.java -classpath "C:\Program Files\Apache Software Foundation\Tomcat 5.5\common\lib\servlet-api.jar"

Once you have compiled a servlet, you must enable Tomcat to find it. This means putting it into a directory under Tomcat's **webapps** directory and entering its name into a **web.xml** file. To keep things simple, the examples in this chapter use the directory and **web.xml** file that Tomcat supplies for its own example servlets. Here is the procedure that you will follow.First, copy the servlet's class file into the following directory:

C:\Program Files\Apache Software Foundation\Tomcat 5.5 \webapps\servlets examples\WEB-INF\classes

Next, add the servlet's name and mapping to the **web.xml** file in the following directory:

C:\Program Files\Apache Software Foundation\Tomcat 5.5\webapps\servlets-examples\WEB-INF.

For instance, assuming the first example, called **HelloServlet**, you will add the following lines in the section that defines the servlets:

```
<servlet>
<servlet-name>HelloServlet</servlet-name>
<servlet-class>HelloServlet</servlet-class>
</servlet>
```

Next, you will add the following lines to the section that defines the servlet mappings.

```
<servlet-mapping>
<servlet-name>HelloServlet</servlet-name>
<url-pattern>/servlet/HelloServlet</url-pattern>
</servlet-mapping>
```

Follow this same general procedure for all of the examples.

6.5. A Simple Servlet

The basic steps are the following:

1) Create and compile the servlet source code. Then, copy the servlet's class file to the proper directory, and add the servlet's name and mappings to the proper **web.xml** file.
2) Start Tomcat.
3) Start a web browser and request the servlet.

Let us examine each of these steps in detail.

Create and Compile the Servlet Source Code

To begin, create a file named **HelloServlet.java** that contains the following program:

```
import java.io.*;
import javax.servlet.*;
public class HelloServlet extends GenericServlet {
public void service(ServletRequest request,
ServletResponse response)
throws ServletException, IOException {
response.setContentType("text/html");
PrintWriter pw = response.getWriter();
pw.println("<B>Hello!");
pw.close();
}
}
```

Start Tomcat

Start Tomcat as explained earlier. Tomcat must be running before you try to execute a servlet.

Start a Web Browser and Request the Servlet

Start a web browser and enter the URL shown here:

http://localhost:8080/servlets-examples/servlet/HelloServlet

Alternatively, you may enter the URL shown here:

http://127.0.0.1:8080/servlets-examples/servlet/HelloServlet

This can be done because 127.0.0.1 is defined as the IP address of the local machine.

The output of the servlet in the browser display area. It will contain the string **Hello!** in bold type.

6.6. The Servlet API

Two packages contain the classes and interfaces that are required to build servlets. These are **javax.servlet** and **javax.servlet. Http**. Packages are standard extensions provided by Tomcat. Therefore, they are not included with Java SE 6.

6.7. The Javax.Servlet Package

The **javax.servlet** package contains a number of interfaces and classes that establish the framework in which servlets operate. The following table summarizes the core interfaces that are provided in this package. The most significant of these is **Servlet.**

All servlets must implement this interface or extend a class that implements the interface. The **ServletRequest** and **ServletResponse** interfaces are also very important.

Interface	Description
Servlet	Declares life cycle methods for a servlet.
ServletConfig	Allows servlets to get initialization parameters.
ServletContext	Enables servlets to log events and access information about their environment.
ServletRequest	Used to read data from a client request.
ServletResponse	Used to write data to a client response.

The following table summarizes the core classes that are provided in the **javax.servlet** package:

Class	Description
GenericServlet	Implements the **Servlet** and **ServletConfig** interfaces.
ServletInputStream	Provides an input stream for reading requests from a client.
ServletOutputStream	Provides an output stream for writing responses to a client.
ServletException	Indicates a servlet error occurred.
UnavailableException	Indicates a servlet is unavailable.

The Servlet Interface: All servlets must implement the **Servlet** interface. It declares the **init( )**, **service( )**, and **destroy( )** methods that are called by the server during the life cycle of a servlet. A method is also provided that allows a servlet to obtain any initialization parameters. The methods defined by **Servlet** are shown in Table below

Method	Description
void destroy( )	Called when the servlet is unloaded.
ServletConfig getServletConfig( )	Returns a **ServletConfig** object that contains any initialization parameters.
String getServletInfo( )	Returns a string describing the servlet.
void init(ServletConfig *sc*) throws ServletException	Called when the servlet is initialized. Initialization parameters for the servlet can be obtained from *sc*. An **UnavailableException** should be thrown if the servlet cannot be initialized.
void service(ServletRequest *req*, ServletResponse *res*) throws ServletException, IOException	Called to process a request from a client. The request from the client can be read from *req*. The response to the client can be written to *res*. An exception is generated if a servlet or IO problem occurs.

The **init( )**, **service( )**, and **destroy( )** methods are the life cycle methods of the servlet. These are invoked by the server. The **getServletConfig( )** method is called by the servlet to obtain initialization parameters. A servlet developer overrides the **getServletInfo( )** method to provide a string with useful information (for example, author, version, date, copyright). This method is also invoked by the server.

The ServletConfig Interface: The **ServletConfig** interface allows a servlet to obtain configuration data when it is loaded. The methods declared by this interface are summarized here:

Method	Description
ServletContext getServletContext( )	Returns the context for this servlet.
String getInitParameter(String *param*)	Returns the value of the initialization parameter named *param*.
Enumeration getInitParameterNames( )	Returns an enumeration of all initialization parameter names.
String getServletName( )	Returns the name of the invoking servlet.

The ServletContext Interface: The **ServletContext** interface enables servlets to obtain information about their environment. Several of its methods are summarized below

Method	Description
Object getAttribute(String *attr*)	Returns the value of the server attribute named *attr*.
String getMimeType(String *file*)	Returns the MIME type of *file*.
String getRealPath(String *vpath*)	Returns the real path that corresponds to the virtual path *vpath*.
String getServerInfo( )	Returns information about the server.
void log(String *s*)	Writes *s* to the servlet log.
void log(String *s*, Throwable *e*)	Writes *s* and the stack trace for *e* to the servlet log.
void setAttribute(String *attr*, Object *val*)	Sets the attribute specified by *attr* to the value passed in *val*.

The ServletRequest Interface: The **ServletRequest** interface enables a servlet to obtain information about a client request. Several of its methods are summarized in Table

Method	Description
Object getAttribute(String *attr*)	Returns the value of the attribute named *attr*.
String getCharacterEncoding( )	Returns the character encoding of the request.
int getContentLength( )	Returns the size of the request. The value –1 is returned if the size is unavailable.
String getContentType( )	Returns the type of the request. A **null** value is returned if the type cannot be determined.
ServletInputStream getInputStream( ) throws IOException	Returns a **ServletInputStream** that can be used to read binary data from the request. An **IllegalStateException** is thrown if **getReader( )** has already been invoked for this request.
String getParameter(String *pname*)	Returns the value of the parameter named *pname*.
Enumeration getParameterNames( )	Returns an enumeration of the parameter names for this request.
String[ ] getParameterValues(String *name*)	Returns an array containing values associated with the parameter specified by *name*.
String getProtocol( )	Returns a description of the protocol.
BufferedReader getReader( ) throws IOException	Returns a buffered reader that can be used to read text from the request. An **IllegalStateException** is thrown if **getInputStream( )** has already been invoked for this request.
String getRemoteAddr( )	Returns the string equivalent of the client IP address.
String getRemoteHost( )	Returns the string equivalent of the client host name.
String getScheme( )	Returns the transmission scheme of the URL used for the request (for example, "http", "ftp").
String getServerName( )	Returns the name of the server.
int getServerPort( )	Returns the port number.

The ServletResponse Interface: The **ServletResponse** interface enables a servlet to formulate a response for a client. Several of its methods are summarized in Table below.

Method	Description
String getCharacterEncoding( )	Returns the character encoding for the response.
ServletOutputStream getOutputStream( ) throws IOException	Returns a **ServletOutputStream** that can be used to write binary data to the response. An **IllegalStateException** is thrown if **getWriter( )** has already been invoked for this request.
PrintWriter getWriter( ) throws IOException	Returns a **PrintWriter** that can be used to write character data to the response. An **IllegalStateException** is thrown if **getOutputStream( )** has already been invoked for this request.
void setContentLength(int *size*)	Sets the content length for the response to *size*.
void setContentType(String *type*)	Sets the content type for the response to *type*.

The GenericServlet Class: The **GenericServlet** class provides implementations of the basic life cycle methods for a servlet. **GenericServlet** implements the **Servlet** and **ServletConfig** interfaces. In addition, a method to append a string to the server log file is available. The signatures of this method are shown here:

void log(String *s*)

void log(String *s*, Throwable *e*)

Here, *s* is the string to be appended to the log, and *e* is an exception that occurred.

The ServletInputStream Class: The **ServletInputStream** class extends **InputStream**. It is implemented by the servlet container and provides an input stream that a servlet developer can use to read the data from a client request. It defines the default constructor. In addition, a method is provided to read bytes from the stream. It is shown here:

int readLine(byte[ ] *buffer*, int *offset*, int *size*) throws IOException

Here, *buffer* is the array into which *size* bytes are placed starting at *offset*. The method returns the actual number of bytes read or –1 if an end-of-stream condition is encountered. **The ServletOutputStream Class:** The **ServletOutputStream** class extends **OutputStream**. It is implemented by the servlet container and provides an output stream that a servlet developer can use to write data to a client response. A default constructor is defined. It also defines the **print( )** and **println( )** methods, which output data to the stream.

The Servlet Exception Classes: javax.servlet defines two exceptions. The first is **ServletException**, which indicates that a servlet problem has occurred. The second is **UnavailableException**, which extends **ServletException**. It indicates that a servlet is unavailable.

6.8. Reading Servlet Parameter

The **ServletRequest** interface includes methods that allow to read the names and values of parameters that are included in a client request. Here is an example of a servlet that illustrates their use. The example contains two files. A web page is defined in **PostParameters. htm**, and a servlet is defined in **PostParametersServlet.java**.

The HTML source code for **PostParameters.htm** is shown in the following listing. It defines a table that contains two labels and two text fields. One of the labels is Employee and the other is Phone. There is also a submit button. Notice that the action parameter of the form tag specifies a URL. The URL identifies the servlet to process the HTTP POST request.

```
<html>
 <body>
  <center>
    <form name="Form1"  method="post" action="http://localhost:8080/servlets-
examples/servlet/PostParametersServlet">
<table>
   <tr>
      <td><B>Employee</td>
      <td><input type=textbox name="e" size="25" value=""></td>
   </tr>
   <tr>
      <td><B>Phone</td>
      <td><input type=textbox name="p" size="25" value=""></td>
  </tr>
</table>
  <input type=submit value="Submit">
 </body>
</html>
```

The source code for **PostParametersServlet.java** is shown in the following listing. The **service( )** method is overridden to process client requests. The **getParameterNames( )** method returns an enumeration of the parameter names. These are processed in a loop. You can see that the parameter name and value are output to the client. The parameter value is obtained via the **getParameter( )** method.

```
import java.io.*;
import java.util.*;
import javax.servlet.*;
public class PostParametersServlet
extends GenericServlet {
public void service(ServletRequest request,
ServletResponse response)
```

```
throws ServletException, IOException {
// Get print writer.
PrintWriter pw = response.getWriter();
// Get enumeration of parameter names.
Enumeration e = request.getParameterNames();
// Display parameter names and values.
while(e.hasMoreElements()) {
String pname = (String)e.nextElement();
pw.print(pname + " = ");
String pvalue = request.getParameter(pname);
pw.println(pvalue);
}
pw.close();
}
}
```

6.9. The Javax.Servlet.Http Package

The **javax.servlet.http** package contains a number of interfaces and classes that are commonly used by servlet developers. The following table summarizes the core interfaces that are provided in this package:

Interface	Description
HttpServletRequest	Enables servlets to read data from an HTTP request.
HttpServletResponse	Enables servlets to write data to an HTTP response.
HttpSession	Allows session data to be read and written.
HttpSessionBindingListener	Informs an object that it is bound to or unbound from a session.

The following table summarizes the core classes that are provided in this package. The most important of these is Http Servlet. Servlet developers typically extend this class in order to process HTTP requests.

Class	Description
Cookie	Allows state information to be stored on a client machine.
HttpServlet	Provides methods to handle HTTP requests and responses.
HttpSessionEvent	Encapsulates a session-changed event.
HttpSessionBindingEvent	Indicates when a listener is bound to or unbound from a session value, or that a session attribute changed.

The HttpServletRequest Interface: The **HttpServletRequest** interface enables a servlet to obtain information about a client request.

The HttpServletResponse Interface: The **HttpServletResponse** interface enables a servlet to formulate an HTTP response to a client. Several constants are defined. These correspond to the different status codes that can be assigned to an HTTP response. For example, **SC_OK** indicates that the HTTP request succeeded, and **SC_NOT_FOUND** indicates that the requested resource is not available.

The HttpSession Interface: The **HttpSession** interface enables a servlet to read and write the state information that is associated with an HTTP session. All of the methods of this Interface throw an **IllegalStateException** if the session has already been invalidated.

The HttpSessionBindingListener Interface: The **HttpSessionBindingListener** interface is implemented by objects that need to be notified when they are bound to or unbound from an HTTP session. The methods that are invoked when an object is bound or unbound are

void valueBound(HttpSessionBindingEvent *e*)

void valueUnbound(HttpSessionBindingEvent *e*)

Here, *e* is the event object that describes the binding.

The Cookie Class: The **Cookie** class encapsulates a cookie. A *cookie* is stored on a client and contains state information. Cookies are valuable for tracking user activities. For example, assume that a user visits an online store. A cookie can save the user's name, address, and other information. The user does not need to enter this data each time he or she visits the store. A servlet can write a cookie to a user's machine via the **addCookie( )** method of the **HttpServletResponse** interface. The data for that cookie is then included in the header of the HTTP response that is sent to the browser. The names and values of cookies are stored on the user's machine.

Some of the information that is saved for each cookie includes the following:

- The name of the cookie
- The value of the cookie
- The expiration date of the cookie
- The domain and path of the cookie

The expiration date determines when this cookie is deleted from the user's machine. If an expiration date is not explicitly assigned to a cookie, it is deleted when the current browser session ends. Otherwise, the cookie is saved in a file on the user's machine. The domain and path of the cookie determine when it is included in the header of an HTTP request. If the user enters a URL whose domain and path match these values, the cookie is then supplied to the Web server. Otherwise, it is not.

There is one constructor for **Cookie**. It has the signature shown here:

Cookie(String *name*, String *value*)

Here, the name and value of the cookie are supplied as arguments to the constructor.

The HttpServlet Class: The **HttpServlet** class extends **GenericServlet.** It is commonly used when developing servlets that receive and process HTTP requests.

The HttpSessionEvent Class: HttpSessionEvent encapsulates session events. It extends **EventObject** and is generated when a change occurs to the session. It defines this constructor:

HttpSessionEvent(HttpSession *session*)

Here, session is the source of the event.

HttpSessionEvent defines one method, **getSession( )**, which is shown here:

HttpSession getSession( )

It returns the session in which the event occurred.

The HttpSessionBindingEvent Class: The **HttpSessionBindingEvent** class extends **HttpSessionEvent**. It is generated when a listener is bound to or unbound from a value in an **HttpSession** object. It is also generated when an attribute is bound or unbound. Here are its constructors:

HttpSessionBindingEvent(HttpSession *session*, String *name*)

HttpSessionBindingEvent(HttpSession *session*, String *name*, Object *val*)

Here, session is the source of the event, and name is the name associated with the object that is being bound or unbound. If an attribute is being bound or unbound, its value is passed in val.

The **getName( )** method obtains the name that is being bound or unbound. It is shown here:

String getName( )

The **getSession( )** method, shown next, obtains the session to which the listener is being bound or unbound:

HttpSession getSession( )

The **getValue( )** method obtains the value of the attribute that is being bound or unbound. It is shown here:

Object getValue( )

6.10. Handling http Requests and Responses

The **HttpServlet** class provides specialized methods that handle the various types of HTTP requests.

A servlet developer typically overrides one of these methods. These methods are

doDelete( ), **doGet( )**, **doHead( )**, **doOptions( )**, **doPost( )**, **doPut( )**, and **doTrace( )**.

The GET and POST requests are commonly used when handling form input

Handling HTTP GET Requests

Here we develop a servlet that handles an HTTP GET request. The servlet is invoked when a form on a web page is submitted. The example contains two files. A web page is defined in **ColorGet.htm**, and a servlet is defined in **ColorGetServlet.java**. The HTML source code for **ColorGet.htm** is shown in the following listing. It defines a form that contains a select element and a submit button.

```
<html>
<body>
<center>
<form name="Form1"
action="http://localhost:8080/servlets-examples/servlet/ColorGetServlet">
<B>Color:</B>
<select name="color" size="1">
<option value="Red">Red</option>
<option value="Green">Green</option>
<option value="Blue">Blue</option>
</select>
<br><br>
<input type=submit value="Submit">
</form>
</body>
</html>
```

The source code for **ColorGetServlet.java** is shown in the following listing. The

doGet( ) method is overridden to process any HTTP GET requests that are sent to this servlet. It uses the **getParameter( )** method of **HttpServletRequest** to obtain the selection that was made by the user. A response is then formulated

```
import java.io.*;
import javax.servlet.*;
import javax.servlet.http.*;
public class ColorGetServlet extends HttpServlet {
public void doGet(HttpServletRequest request,
HttpServletResponse response)
throws ServletException, IOException {
String color = request.getParameter("color");
response.setContentType("text/html");
PrintWriter pw = response.getWriter();
pw.println("<B>The selected color is: ");
pw.println(color);
pw.close();
}
}
```

6.11. Using Cookies

Cookies are text files stored on the client computer and they are kept for various information tracking purpose. Java Servlets transparently supports HTTP cookies.

There are three steps involved in identifying returning users:

- Server script sends a set of cookies to the browser. For example name, age, or identification number etc.
- Browser stores this information on local machine for future use.
- When next time browser sends any request to web server then it sends those cookies information to the server and server uses that information to identify the user.

Servlet Cookies Methods

public void setDomain(String pattern): This method sets the domain to which cookie applies, for example dbit.co.in

public String getDomain(): This method gets the domain to which cookie applies, for example dbit.co.in

public void setMaxAge(int expiry): This method sets how much time (in seconds) should elapse before the cookie expires. If you don't set this, the cookie will last only for the current session.

public int getMaxAge(): This method returns the maximum age of the cookie, specified in seconds, By default, -1 indicating the cookie will persist until browser shutdown.

public String getName(): This method returns the name of the cookie. The name cannot be changed after creation.

public void setValue(String newValue): This method sets the value associated with the cookie.

public String getValue(): This method gets the value associated with the cookie.

public void setPath(String uri): This method sets the path to which this cookie applies. If you don't specify a path, the cookie is returned for all URLs in the same directory as the current page as well as all subdirectories.

public String getPath(): This method gets the path to which this cookie applies.

The HTML source code for **AddCookie.htm** is shown in the following listing.

This page contains a text field in which a value can be entered. There is also a submit button on the page.

When this button is pressed, the value in the text field is sent to **AddCookieServlet** via an HTTP POST request.

```
<html>
<body>
<center>
<form name="Form1"
method="post"
action="http://localhost:8080/servlets-examples/servlet/AddCookieServlet">
<B>Enter a value for MyCookie:</B>
<input type=textbox name="data" size=25 value="">
<input type=submit value="Submit">
</form>
</body>
</html>
```

The source code for AddCookieServlet.java is shown in the following listing. It gets the value of the parameter named "data". It then creates a Cookie object that has the name "MyCookie" and contains the value of the "data" parameter. The cookie is then added to the header of the HTTP response via the addCookie( ) method. A feedback message is then written to the browser.

```
import java.io.*;
import javax.servlet.*;
import javax.servlet.http.*;
public class AddCookieServlet extends HttpServlet {
public void doPost(HttpServletRequest request,
HttpServletResponse response)
throws ServletException, IOException {
// Get parameter from HTTP request.
String data = request.getParameter("data");
// Create cookie.
Cookie cookie = new Cookie("MyCookie", data);
// Add cookie to HTTP response.
response.addCookie(cookie);
// Write output to browser.
response.setContentType("text/html");
PrintWriter pw = response.getWriter();
pw.println("<B>MyCookie has been set to");
pw.println(data);
pw.close();
}
}
```

The source code for GetCookiesServlet.java is shown in the following listing. It invokes the getCookies( ) method to read any cookies that are included in the HTTP GET request. The names and values of these cookies are then written to the HTTP response. Observe that the getName( ) and getValue( ) methods are called to obtain this information.

```
import java.io.*;
import javax.servlet.*;
import javax.servlet.http.*;
public class GetCookiesServlet extends HttpServlet {
public void doGet(HttpServletRequest request,
HttpServletResponse response)
```

```
throws ServletException, IOException {
// Get cookies from header of HTTP request.
Cookie[] cookies = request.getCookies();
// Display these cookies.
response.setContentType("text/html");
PrintWriter pw = response.getWriter();
pw.println("<B>");
for(int i = 0; i < cookies.length; i++) {
String name = cookies[i].getName();
String value = cookies[i].getValue();
pw.println("name = " + name +
"; value = " + value);
}
pw.close();
}
}
```

6.12. Session Tracking

HTTP is a stateless protocol. Each request is independent of the previous one. However, in some applications, it is necessary to save state information so that information can be collected from several interactions between a browser and a server. Sessions provide such a mechanism.

A session can be created via the **getSession( )** method of **HttpServletRequest**. An **HttpSession** object is returned. This object can store a set of bindings that associate names with objects. The **setAttribute( )**, **getAttribute( )**, **getAttributeNames( )**, and **removeAttribute( )** methods of **HttpSession** manage these bindings. It is important to note that session state is shared among all the servlets that are associated with a particular client.

The following servlet illustrates how to use session state. The **getSession( )** method gets the current session. A new session is created if one does not already exist. The **getAttribute( )** method is called to obtain the object that is bound to the name "date". That object is a **Date** object that encapsulates the date and time when this page was last accessed. (Of course, there is no such binding when the page is first accessed.) A **Date** object encapsulating the current date and time is then created. The **setAttribute( )** method is called to bind the name "date" to this object.

```
import java.io.*;
import java.util.*;
import javax.servlet.*;
import javax.servlet.http.*;
public class DateServlet extends HttpServlet {
public void doGet(HttpServletRequest request,
HttpServletResponse response)
throws ServletException, IOException {
// Get the HttpSession object.
HttpSession hs = request.getSession(true);
// Get writer.
response.setContentType("text/html");
PrintWriter pw = response.getWriter();
pw.print("<B>");
// Display date/time of last access.
Date date = (Date)hs.getAttribute("date");
if(date != null) {
pw.print("Last access: " + date + "<br>");
}
// Display current date/time.
date = new Date();
hs.setAttribute("date", date);
pw.println("Current date: " + date);
}
}
```

6.13. Questions

1. What are servlets? Briefly explain the application of servlets in web programming.
2. Explain the life cycle of servlet.
3. Write a JAVA servlet which reads two parameters from the webpage, say value 1 and value 2, which are of type integers , and finds the sum of the two values , and return back the result as a webpages.
4. Provide the JAVA syntax for the following:
   i. Handling HTTP request and responses
   ii. Using cookies.

iii. Session tracking.

5. Describe in detail how tomcat web server is configured for development of servlet.
6. With code snippet? Explain how session tracking is handled in java with servlet.
7. List and explain core classes that are provided in Javax.servleet package.
8. Write a program using servlet which contains HTML page to accept username and display greeting message as "Hello username, How are you?" in the browser window.
9. Briefly explain servlet interface, Generic Servlet class and Cookie class.
10. Illustrate the use of session information in servlets.
11. How servlets are better in comparsion with CGI? Explain init() and service().
12. Enlist core classes and interfaces available in javax.servlet.http package.
13. Write a program using servlet which contains HTML page with various color options. When user choose the particular color. The background of that page should be Changed accordingly.
14. List out the difference between CGI and servlet.
15. What is cookie? List out the methods defined by cookie. Write a program in HTML for adding a cookie.

UNIT–7

JSP, RMI

7.1. Java Server Pages (JSP)

JavaServer Pages (JSP) is a technology for developing web pages that support dynamic content which helps developers insert java code in HTML pages by making use of special JSP tags, most of which start with <% and end with %>.

A JavaServer Pages component is a type of Java servlet that is designed to fulfill the role of a user interface for a Java web application. Web developers write JSPs as text files that combine HTML or XHTML code, XML elements, and embedded JSP actions and commands.

Using JSP, you can collect input from users through web page forms, present records from a database or another source, and create web pages dynamically.

JSP tags can be used for a variety of purposes, such as retrieving information from a database or registering user preferences, accessing JavaBeans components, passing control between pages and sharing information between requests, pages etc.

JSP Architecture: The web server needs a JSP engine i.e. container to process JSP pages. The JSP container is responsible for intercepting requests for JSP pages. This tutorial makes use of Apache which has built-in JSP container to support JSP pages development.

A JSP container works with the Web server to provide the runtime environment and other services a JSP needs. It knows how to understand the special elements that are part of JSPs.

Following diagram shows the position of JSP container and JSP files in a Web Application.

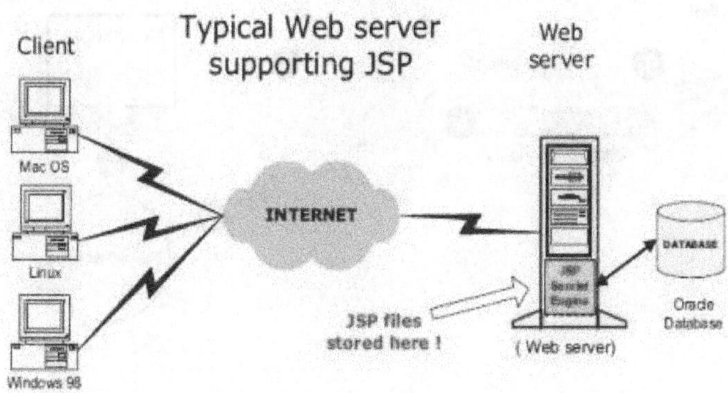

JSP Processing: The following steps explain how the web server creates the web page using JSP:

- As with a normal page, your browser sends an HTTP request to the web server.
- The web server recognizes that the HTTP request is for a JSP page and forwards it to a JSP engine. This is done by using the URL or JSP page which ends with **.jsp** instead of .html.
- The JSP engine loads the JSP page from disk and converts it into a servlet content. This conversion is very simple in which all template text is converted to println( ) statements and all JSP elements are converted to Java code that implements the corresponding dynamic behavior of the page.
- The JSP engine compiles the servlet into an executable class and forwards the original request to a servlet engine.
- A part of the web server called the servlet engine loads the Servlet class and executes it. During execution, the servlet produces an output in HTML format, which the servlet engine passes to the web server inside an HTTP response.
- The web server forwards the HTTP response to your browser in terms of static HTML content.
- Finally web browser handles the dynamically generated HTML page inside the HTTP response exactly as if it were a static page.

All the above mentioned steps can be shown below in the following diagram:

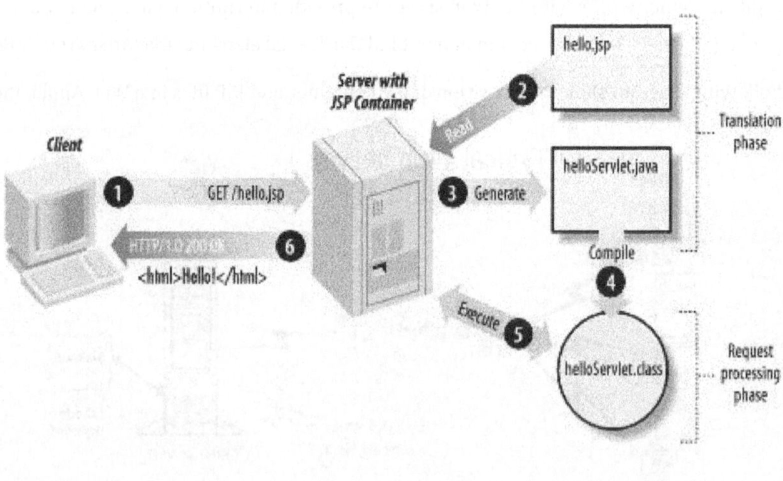

7.2. Request String

We may come across many situations when we need to pass some information from the browser to web server and ultimately to backend program. The browser uses two methods to pass this information to web server. These methods are GET Method and POST Method.

GET Method

The GET method sends the encoded user information appended to the page request. The page and the encoded information are separated by the ? character as follows:

http://www.test.com/hello?key1=value1&key2=value2

1) The GET method is the default method to pass information from browser to web server and it produces a long string that appears in your browser's Location: box.
2) Never use the GET method if you have password or other sensitive information to pass to the server.
3) The GET method has size limitation: only 1024 characters can be in a request string.

This information is passed using QUERY_STRING header and will be accessible through QUERY_STRING environment variable which can be handled using getQueryString() and getParameter() methods of request object.

POST Method

A generally more reliable method of passing information to a backend program is the POST method. This method packages the information in exactly the same way as GET methods, but instead of sending it as a text string after a? in the URL it sends it as a separate message. This message comes to the backend program in the form of the standard input which you can parse and use for your processing.

JSP handles this type of requests using getParameter() method to read simple parameters and getInputStream() method to read binary data stream coming from the client.

Reading Form Data using JSP

JSP handles form data parsing automatically using the following methods depending on the situation:

1) **getParameter():** You call request.getParameter() method to get the value of a form parameter.
2) **getParameterValues():** Call this method if the parameter appears more than once and returns multiple values, for example checkbox.

3) **getParameterNames():** Call this method if you want a complete list of all parameters in the current request.
4) **getInputStream():** Call this method to read binary data stream coming from the client.

GET Method Example Using URL

Below is **main.jsp** JSP program to handle input given by web browser. We are going to use **getParameter()** method which makes it very easy to access passed information:

Main.jsp

```
<html>
<head>
<title>Using GET Method to Read Form Data</title>
</head>
<body>
<center>
<h1>Using GET Method to Read Form Data</h1>
<ul>
<li><p><b>First Name:</b>
  <%= request.getParameter("first_name")%>
</p></li>
<li><p><b>Last  Name:</b>
  <%= request.getParameter("last_name")%>
</p></li>
</ul>
</body>
</html>
```

GET Method Example Using Form

Here is a simple example which passes two values using HTML FORM and submit button. We are going to use same JSP main.jsp to handle this input.

Main.html

```
<html>
<body>
<form action="main.jsp" method="GET">
First Name: <input type="text" name="first_name">
```

```
<br />
Last Name: <input type="text" name="last_name" />
<input type="submit" value="Submit" />
</form>
</body>
</html>
```

POST Method Example Using Form

main.jsp

```
<html>
<head>
<title>Using GET and POST Method to Read Form Data</title>
</head>
<body>
<center>
<h1>Using GET Method to Read Form Data</h1>
<ul>
<li><p><b>First Name:</b>
  <%= request.getParameter("first_name")%>
</p></li>
<li><p><b>Last  Name:</b>
  <%= request.getParameter("last_name")%>
</p></li>
</ul>
</body>
</html>
```

Main.html

```
<html>
<body>
<form action="main.jsp" method="POST">
First Name: <input type="text" name="first_name">
<br />
Last Name: <input type="text" name="last_name" />
<input type="submit" value="Submit" />
```

```
</form>
</body>
</html>
```

Reading All Form Parameters

Following is the generic example which uses **getParameterNames()** method of HttpServletRequest to read all the available from parameters. This method returns an Enumeration that contains the parameter names in an unspecified order.

Once we have an Enumeration, we can loop down the Enumeration in the standard manner, using *hasMoreElements()* method to determine when to stop and using *nextElement()* method to get each parameter name.

```
<%@ page import="java.io.*,java.util.*" %>
<html>
<head>
<title>HTTP Header Request Example</title>
</head>
<body>
<center>
<h2>HTTP Header Request Example</h2>
<table width="100%" border="1" align="center">
<tr bgcolor="#949494">
<th>Param Name</th><th>Param Value(s)</th>
</tr>
<%
  Enumeration paramNames = request.getParameterNames();
  while(paramNames.hasMoreElements()) {
    String paramName = (String)paramNames.nextElement();
    out.print("<tr><td>" + paramName + "</td>\n");
    String paramValue = request.getHeader(paramName);
    out.println("<td> " + paramValue + "</td></tr>\n");
  }
%>
</table>
</center>
```

```
</body>
</html>
```

Following is the content of Hello.htm:

```
<html>
<body>
<form action="main.jsp" method="POST" target="_blank">
<input type="checkbox" name="maths" checked="checked" /> Maths
<input type="checkbox" name="physics" /> Physics
<input type="checkbox" name="chemistry" checked="checked" /> Chem
<input type="submit" value="Select Subject" />
</form>
</body>
</html>
```

7.3. User Sessions

HTTP is a "stateless" protocol which means each time a client retrieves a Web page, the client opens a separate connection to the Web server and the server automatically does not keep any record of previous client request. Still there are following three ways to maintain session between web client and web server:

1) **Cookies:** A webserver can assign a unique session ID as a cookie to each web client and for subsequent requests from the client they can be recognized using the received cookie.

   This may not be an effective way because many time browsers does not support a cookie, so it is better not to use this procedure to maintain the sessions.

2) **Hidden Form Fields:** A web server can send a hidden HTML form field along with a unique session ID as follows:

   ```
   <input type="hidden" name="sessionid" value="12345">
   ```

   This entry means that, when the form is submitted, the specified name and value are automatically included in the GET or POST data. Each time when web browser sends request back, then session_id value can be used to keep the track of different web browsers.

   This could be an effective way of keeping track of the session but clicking on a regular (<A HREF...>) hypertext link does not result in a form submission, so hidden form fields also cannot support general session tracking.

3) **URL Rewriting:** You can append some extra data on the end of each URL that identifies the session, and the server can associate that session identifier with data it has stored about that session.

   For example, with http://dbit.co.in/file1.htm;sessionid=12345, the session identifier is attached as sessionid=12345 which can be accessed at the web server to identify the client.

   URL rewriting is a better way to maintain sessions and works for the browsers when they don't support cookies but here drawback is that you would have generate every URL dynamically to assign a session ID though page is simple static HTML page.

4) **The session Object:** Apart from the above mentioned three ways, JSP makes use of servlet provided Http Session Interface which provides a way to identify a user across more than one page request or visit to a Web site and to store information about that user.

   By default, JSPs have session tracking enabled and a new HttpSession object is instantiated for each new client automatically. Disabling session tracking requires explicitly turning it off by setting the page directive session attribute to false as follows:

   <%@ page session="false" %>

   The JSP engine exposes the HttpSession object to the JSP author through the implicit session object. Since session object is already provided to the JSP programmer, the programmer can immediately begin storing and retrieving data from the object without any initialization or getSession().

   Here is a summary of important methods available through session object:

   public Object getAttribute(String name) : This method returns the object bound with the specified name in this session, or null if no object is bound under the name.

   public Enumeration getAttributeNames(): This method returns an Enumeration of String objects containing the names of all the objects bound to this session.

   public long getCreationTime(): This method returns the time when this session was created, measured in milliseconds since midnight January 1, 1970 GMT.

   public String getId(): This method returns a string containing the unique identifier assigned to this session.

   public long getLastAccessedTime(): This method returns the last time the client sent a request associated with this session, as the number of milliseconds since midnight January 1, 1970 GMT.

public int getMaxInactiveInterval(): This method returns the maximum time interval, in seconds, that the servlet container will keep this session open between client accesses.

public void removeAttribute(String name): This method removes the object bound with the specified name from this session.

public void setAttribute(String name, Object value) :This method binds an object to this session, using the name specified.

public void setMaxInactiveInterval(int interval): This method specifies the time, in seconds, between client requests before the servlet container will invalidate this session.

5) **Session Tracking Example:** This example describes how to use the HttpSession object to find out the creation time and the last-accessed time for a session. We would associate a new session with the request if one does not already exist

```
<%@ page import="java.io.*,java.util.*" %>
<%
  // Get session creation time.
  Date createTime = new Date(session.getCreationTime());
  // Get last access time of this web page.
  Date lastAccessTime = new Date(session.getLastAccessedTime());
  String title = "Welcome Back to my website";
  Integer visitCount = new Integer(0);
  String visitCountKey = new String("visitCount");
  String userIDKey = new String("userID");
  String userID = new String("ABCD");
  // Check if this is new comer on your web page.
  if (session.isNew()){
    title = "Welcome to my website";
    session.setAttribute(userIDKey, userID);
    session.setAttribute(visitCountKey,  visitCount);
  }
  visitCount = (Integer)session.getAttribute(visitCountKey);
  visitCount = visitCount + 1;
  userID = (String)session.getAttribute(userIDKey);
  session.setAttribute(visitCountKey,  visitCount);
%>
<html>
```

```
<head>
<title>Session Tracking</title>
</head>
<body>
<center>
<h1>Session Tracking</h1>
</center>
<table border="1" align="center">
<tr bgcolor="#949494">
  <th>Session info</th>
  <th>Value</th>
</tr>
<tr>
  <td>id</td>
  <td><% out.print( session.getId()); %></td>
</tr>
<tr>
  <td>Creation Time</td>
  <td><% out.print(createTime); %></td>
</tr>
<tr>
  <td>Time of Last Access</td>
  <td><% out.print(lastAccessTime); %></td>
</tr>
<tr>
  <td>User ID</td>
  <td><% out.print(userID); %></td>
</tr>
<tr>
  <td>Number of visits</td>
  <td><% out.print(visitCount); %></td>
</tr>
</table>
</body>
</html>
```

7.4. Cookies

Cookies are text files stored on the client computer and they are kept for various information tracking purpose. JSP transparently supports HTTP cookies using underlying servlet technology. There are three steps involved in identifying returning users:

1) Server script sends a set of cookies to the browser. For example name, age, or identification number etc.
2) Browser stores this information on local machine for future use.
3) When next time browser sends any request to web server then it sends those cookies information to the server and server uses that information to identify the user or may be for some other purpose as well.

A JSP script will have access to the cookies through the request method *request.getCookies ()* which returns an array of *Cookie* objects.

Following is the list of useful methods associated with Cookie object which you can use while manipulating cookies in JSP:

public void setDomain(String pattern): This method sets the domain to which cookie applies, for example dbit.co.in

public String getDomain(): This method gets the domain to which cookie applies, for example dbit.co.in

public void setMaxAge(int expiry): This method sets how much time (in seconds) should elapse before the cookie expires. If you don't set this, the cookie will last only for the current session.

public int getMaxAge(): This method returns the maximum age of the cookie, specified in seconds, By default, -1 indicating the cookie will persist until browser shutdown.

public String getName(): This method returns the name of the cookie. The name cannot be changed after creation.

public void setValue(String newValue): This method sets the value associated with the cookie.

public String getValue(): This method gets the value associated with the cookie.

public void setPath(String uri): This method sets the path to which this cookie applies. If you don't specify a path, the cookie is returned for all URLs in the same directory as the current page as well as all subdirectories.

public String getPath(): This method gets the path to which this cookie applies.

Setting Cookies with JSP: Setting cookies with JSP involves three steps:

1. **Creating a Cookie object:** You call the Cookie constructor with a cookie name and a cookie value, both of which are strings.

   ```
   Cookie cookie = new Cookie("key","value");
   ```

   Keep in mind; neither the name nor the value should contain white space or any of the following characters:

   [ ] ( ) = , " / ? @ : ;

2. **Setting the maximum age:** You use setMaxAge to specify how long (in seconds) the cookie should be valid. Following would set up a cookie for 24 hours.

   ```
   cookie.setMaxAge(60*60*24);
   ```

3. **Sending the Cookie into the HTTP response headers:** You use **response.addCookie** to add cookies in the HTTP response header as follows:

   ```
   response.addCookie(cookie);
   ```

Example: cookie.jsp

```
<%
  // Create cookies for first and last names.
  Cookie firstName = new Cookie("first_name",
                              request.getParameter("first_name"));
  Cookie lastName = new Cookie("last_name",
                              request.getParameter("last_name"));
  // Set expiry date after 24 Hrs for both the cookies.
  firstName.setMaxAge(60*60*24);
  lastName.setMaxAge(60*60*24);
  // Add both the cookies in the response header.
  response.addCookie( firstName );
  response.addCookie( lastName );
%>
<html>
<head>
<title>Setting Cookies</title>
</head>
<body>
<center>
```

```
<h1>Setting Cookies</h1>
</center>
<ul>
<li><p><b>First Name:</b>
  <%= request.getParameter ("first_name")%>
</p></li>
<li><p><b>Last  Name:</b>
  <%= request.getParameter("last_name")%>
</p></li>
</ul>
</body>
</html>
Main.html
<html>
<body>
<form action="cookie.jsp" method="GET">
First Name: <input type="text" name="first_name">
<br />
Last Name: <input type="text" name="last_name" />
<input type="submit" value="Submit" />
</form>
</body>
</html>
```

Reading Cookies with JSP

To read cookies, you need to create an array of javax.servlet.http.Cookie objects by calling the getCookies( ) method of HttpServletRequest. Then cycle through the array, and use getName() and getValue() methods to access each cookie and associated value.

Example

Let us read cookies which we have set in previous example:

```
<html>
<head>
<title>Reading Cookies</title>
</head>
```

```
<body>
<center>
<h1>Reading Cookies</h1>
</center>
<%
 Cookie cookie = null;
 Cookie[] cookies = null;
 // Get an array of Cookies associated with this domain
 cookies = request.getCookies();
 if( cookies != null ){
   out.println("<h2> Found Cookies Name and Value</h2>");
   for (int i = 0; i < cookies.length; i++){
     cookie = cookies[i];
     out.print("Name : " + cookie.getName( ) + ", ");
     out.print("Value: " + cookie.getValue( )+" <br/>");
   }
 }else{
   out.println("<h2>No cookies founds</h2>");
 }
%>
</body>
</html>
```

7.5. Questions

1. Mention the purpose of use of JSP and JAVA RMI.
2. Explain any four JSP tags. Demonstrate with a simple JSP program.
3. Briefly explain the working of JAVA RMI programs, by mentioning its steps.
4. What are the differences between server side and client side JAVA RMI?
5. What is RMI? Describe the code snippet RMI at a client side.
6. Write a JSP to create and read cookie named user id that Stores a value JB0007.
7. What is RMI? Describe with code snippet RMI at server side.
8. Define JSP. Explain the two tppes of control statements used in JSP by taking a suitable examples?
9. Write a JSP Program to create and read a cookie called "EMPID" that has a value of AN2356.

10. Department has set the grade for the subject Java as follows: Above 90=A , 80-89 = B, 70-79 = C Below 70= fail. Sham enters his marks for The subject Java in the interface provided. Write a jsp program that accept the marks entered and display his grade to the browser.
11. What are the advantages of JSP?
12. Write a program using RMI concept such as client and server program in which Client sends hello message to server and server replies for the client.
13. Write the difference between JSP and Servlets.

UNIT-8

JAVA BEANS

Introduction

The EJB specification intends to provide a standard way to implement the back-end 'business' code typically found in enterprise applications (as opposed to 'front-end' interface code). Such code addresses the same types of problems, and solutions to these problems are often repeatedly re-implemented by programmers.

Enterprise JavaBeans is intended to handle such common concerns as persistence, transactional integrity, and security in a standard way, leaving programmers free to concentrate on the particular problem at hand.

8.1. Objectives

To learn the concepts of Enterprise java beans an IDE. To deploy descriptors, the session java bean, entity java bean, message driven bean.

8.2. Enterprise Java Beans

Definition : Enterprise JavaBeans™ (EJB) is a managed, server-side component architecture or modular construction of enterprise applications. In a typical J2EE application, Enterprise JavaBeans (EJBs) contain the application's business logic and live business data.

Although it is possible to use standard Java objects to contain your business logic and business data, using EJBs addresses many of the issues you would find by using simple Java objects, such as scalability, lifecycle management, and state management. There are three different types of EJB that are suited to different purposes:

1) **Session EJB**: A Session EJB is useful for mapping business process flow (or equivalent application concepts). There are two sub-types of Session EJB — stateless and state ful represent "pure" functionality that is created as it is needed.
2) **Entity EJB**: An Entity EJB maps a combination of data (or equivalent application concept) and associated functionality. Entity EJBs are usually based on an underlying data store and will be created based on that data within it.
3) **Message-driven EJB**: A Message-driven EJB is very similar in concept to a Session EJB, but is only activated when an asynchronous message arrives.

8.3. Deployment Descriptors

Definition: A deployment descriptor is a file that defines the following kinds of information:

EJB structural information, such as the EJB name, class, home and remote interfaces, bean type (session or entity), environment entries, resource factory references, EJB references, security role references, as well as additional information based on the bean type.

Application assembly information, such as EJB references, security roles, security role references, method permissions, and container transaction attributes. Specifying assembly descriptor information is an optional task that an Application Assembler performs.

8.4. Session Bean

1) Session bean is a type of enterprise bean; a type of EJB server-side component.
2) Session bean components implement the javax.ejb. Session Bean interface and can be stateless or stateful.
3) Stateless session beans are components that perform transient services; stateful session beans are components that are dedicated to one client and act as a server-side extension of that client. Session beans can act as agents modeling workflow or provide access to special transient business services. As an agent, a stateful session bean might represent a customer's session at an online shopping site.
4) As a transitive service, a stateless session bean might provide access to validate and Process credit card orders.
5) Session beans do not normally represent persistent business concepts like Employee or Order. This is the domain of a different component type called an entity bean.

Example :package ejb.demo;

```
import javax.ejb.*;
import java.rmi.Remote;
import java.rmi.RemoteException; import java.util. *;
/**
* This interface is extremely simple it declares only * one create method.
*/
public interface DemoHome extends EJBHome {
public Demo create() throws CreateException, RemoteException;
}
```

8.5. Entity Java Bean

1) An entity bean represents a business object in a persistent storage mechanism.
2) Some examples of business objects are customers, orders, and products.
3) In the J2EE SDK, the persistent storage mechanism is a relational database.
4) Typically, each entity bean has an underlying table in a relational database, and each instance of the bean corresponds to a row in that table.

8.6. Message-Driven Bean

1) A message-driven bean is an enterprise bean that allows J2EE applications to process messages asynchronously.
2) It acts as a JMS message listener, which is similar to an event listener except that it receives messages instead of events.
3) The messages may be sent by any J2EE component--an application client, another enterprise bean, or a Web component--or by a JMS application or system that does not use J2EE technology. Message-driven beans currently process only JMS messages, but in the future they may be used to process other kinds of messages.

8.7. The JAR File

The Java Archive (JAR) file format enables you to bundle multiple files into a single archive file. Typically a JAR file contains the class files and auxiliary resources associated with applets and applications.

The JAR file format provides many benefits:

1) Security: You can digitally sign the contents of a JAR file. Users who recognize your signature can then optionally grant your software security privileges it wouldn't otherwise have.
2) Decreased download time: If your applet is bundled in a JAR file, the applet's class files and associated resources can be downloaded to a browser in a single HTTP transaction without the need for opening a new connection for each file.
3) Compression: The JAR format allows you to compress your files for efficient storage.
4) Packaging for extensions: The extensions framework provides a means by which you can add functionality to the Java core platform, and the JAR file format defines the packaging for extensions. By using the JAR file format, you can turn your software into extensions as well.

5) Package Sealing: Packages stored in JAR files can be optionally sealed so that the package can enforce version consistency. Sealing a package within a JAR file means that all classes defined in that package must be found in the same JAR file.
6) Package Versioning: A JAR file can hold data about the files it contains, such as vendor and version information.
7) Portability: The mechanism for handling JAR files is a standard part of the Java platform's core API.

8.8. Course Outcomes

1) Ability to execute a java program using the java beans developed concepts.

